Presented to

Evan Lowell Sprague

By

_____

On the Occasion of

_____

Date

_____

THE BIBLE PROMISE BOOK

KING JAMES VERSION

PUBLISHING, INC.
Uhrichsville, Ohio

Compiled by Sam Wellman and Jennifer Hahn.

Published by Barbour Publishing, Inc., P.O. Box 719, Uhrichsville, OH 44683, http://www.barbourbooks.com

 Member of the
Evangelical Christian
Publishers Association

Printed in the United States of America.

INTRODUCTION

Our world sends many conflicting signals on the important issues of life. How should we approach anger? Is discipline a good thing, or not? Why speak with honesty? Is prayer for real? What is true wisdom?

In His kindness, God has answered all of these questions—and many more—in the pages of His Word, the Bible. Whatever our needs, we can find in Scripture the principles we need to address the issues we face.

This collection of Bible verses is a handy reference to some of the key issues that all people—and especially men—face. In these pages, you'll find carefully selected verses that address topics like adversity, courage, family discipline, duty, labor, prayer, and temptation. In fact, more than five dozen categories are covered, arranged alphabetically for ease of use.

This book is not intended to replace regular, personal Bible study. Nor is it a replacement for a good concordance for in-depth study of a particular subject. It is, however, a quick reference to some of the key issues of life that men most often face. We hope it will be an encouragement to you as you read.

All Scripture is taken from the King James Version of the Bible.

Contents

EXTRAORDINARY AFFLICTIONS
ARE NOT ALWAYS
THE PUNISHMENT OF
EXTRAORDINARY SINS,
BUT SOMETIMES THE TRIAL OF
EXTRAORDINARY GRACES.

Matthew Henry

That the trial of your faith, being much more precious than of gold that perisheth, though it be tried with fire, might be found unto praise and honour and glory at the appearing of Jesus Christ.

1 PETER 1:7

The righteous cry, and the LORD heareth, and delivereth them out of all their troubles.

PSALM 34:17

But the God of all grace, who hath called us unto his eternal glory by Christ Jesus, after that ye have suffered a while, make you perfect, stablish, strengthen, settle you.   1 PETER 5:10

Blessed are ye, when men shall hate you, and when they shall separate you from their company, and shall reproach you, and cast out your name as evil, for the Son of man's sake.   LUKE 6:22

Though he fall, he shall not be utterly cast down: for the LORD upholdeth him with his hand.
                                                        PSALM 37:24

For this is thankworthy, if a man for conscience toward God endure grief, suffering wrongfully. . . .
  For even hereunto were ye called: because Christ also suffered for us, leaving us an example, that ye should follow his steps:
  Who did no sin, neither was guile found in his mouth:
  Who, when he was reviled, reviled not again; when he suffered, he threatened not; but committed himself to him that judgeth righteously.
                                          1 PETER 2:19, 21–23

For as the sufferings of Christ abound in us, so our consolation also aboundeth by Christ.
  And whether we be afflicted, it is for your consolation and salvation, which is effectual in the enduring of the same sufferings which we also suffer: or whether we be comforted, it is for your consolation and salvation.   2 CORINTHIANS 1:5–6

For I reckon that the sufferings of this present time are not worthy to be compared with the glory which shall be revealed in us. ROMANS 8:18

If ye be reproached for the name of Christ, happy are ye; for the spirit of glory and of God resteth upon you: on their part he is evil spoken of, but on your part he is glorified. 1 PETER 4:14

IS ANY AMONG YOU AFFLICTED? LET HIM PRAY.

James 5:13

These things I have spoken unto you, that in me ye might have peace. In the world ye shall have tribulation: but be of good cheer; I have overcome the world. JOHN 16:33

But the salvation of the righteous is of the LORD: he is their strength in the time of trouble.

PSALM 37:39

But rejoice, inasmuch as ye are partakers of Christ's sufferings; that, when his glory shall be revealed, ye may be glad also with exceeding joy. 1 PETER 4:13

For our light affliction, which is but for a moment, worketh for us a far more exceeding and eternal weight of glory. 2 CORINTHIANS 4:17

ANGER

HE BEST KEEPS FROM
ANGER WHO REMEMBERS
THAT GOD IS
ALWAYS LOOKING UPON HIM.

Plato

He that is slow to wrath is of great understanding: but he that is hasty of spirit exalteth folly.

PROVERBS 14:29

Wherefore, my beloved brethren, let every man be swift to hear, slow to speak, slow to wrath:

For the wrath of man worketh not the righteousness of God.　　　　　　JAMES 1:19–20

It is better to dwell in the wilderness, than with a contentious and an angry woman.　　PROVERBS 21:19

Make no friendship with an angry man; and with a furious man thou shalt not go:

Lest thou learn his ways, and get a snare to thy soul.　　　　　　　　　PROVERBS 22:24–25

Fathers, provoke not your children to anger, lest they be discouraged.　　　　　COLOSSIANS 3:21

A soft answer turneth away wrath: but grievous words stir up anger.　　　　　　　　PROVERBS 15:1

But I say unto you, That whosoever is angry with his brother without a cause shall be in danger of the judgment: and whosoever shall say to his brother, Raca, shall be in danger of the council: but whosoever shall say, Thou fool, shall be in danger of hell fire.　　　　　　　　　　　MATTHEW 5:22

Do all things without murmurings and disputings.
　　　　　　　　　　　PHILIPPIANS 2:14

BE NOT HASTY
IN THY SPIRIT
TO BE ANGRY:
FOR ANGER RESTETH IN
THE BOSOM OF FOOLS.

Ecclesiastes 7:9

A wrathful man stirreth up strife: but he that is slow to anger appeaseth strife.　　　PROVERBS 15:18

He that is slow to anger is better than the mighty; and he that ruleth his spirit than he that taketh a city.   PROVERBS 16:32

Dearly beloved, avenge not yourselves, but rather give place unto wrath: for it is written, Vengeance is mine; I will repay, saith the Lord.   ROMANS 12:19

Better is a dry morsel, and quietness therewith, than an house full of sacrifices with strife.
                                        PROVERBS 17:1

Be ye angry, and sin not: let not the sun go down upon your wrath.   EPHESIANS 4:26

IF A PERSON GETS
HIS ATTITUDE TOWARD MONEY
STRAIGHT,
IT WILL HELP
STRAIGHTEN OUT
ALMOST EVERY OTHER
AREA IN HIS LIFE.

Billy Graham

For which of you, intending to build a tower, sitteth not down first, and counteth the cost, whether he have sufficient to finish it?

Lest haply, after he hath laid the foundation, and is not able to finish it, all that behold it begin to mock him,

Saying, This man began to build, and was not able to finish.   LUKE 14:28–30

A good man leaveth an inheritance to his children's children: and the wealth of the sinner is laid up for the just.   PROVERBS 13:22

There is treasure to be desired and oil in the dwelling of the wise; but a foolish man spendeth it up.
                                    PROVERBS 21:20

And he saith unto them, Whose is this image and superscription?

They say unto him, Caesar's. Then saith he unto them, Render therefore unto Caesar the things which are Caesar's; and unto God the things that are God's.
                                    MATTHEW 22:20–21

And I say unto you, Make to yourselves friends of the mammon of unrighteousness; that, when ye fail, they may receive you into everlasting habitations.

He that is faithful in that which is least is faithful also in much: and he that is unjust in the least is unjust also in much.

If therefore ye have not been faithful in the unrighteous mammon, who will commit to your trust the true riches?

And if ye have not been faithful in that which is another man's, who shall give you that which is your own?

No servant can serve two masters: for either he will hate the one, and love the other; or else he will hold to the one, and despise the other. Ye cannot serve God and mammon.   LUKE 16:9–13

A gracious woman retaineth honour: and strong men retain riches. PROVERBS 11:16

He that loveth pleasure shall be a poor man: he that loveth wine and oil shall not be rich.
PROVERBS 21:17

THE RICH RULETH OVER THE POOR, AND THE BORROWER IS SERVANT TO THE LENDER.
Proverbs 22:7

Be not thou one of them that strike hands, or of them that are sureties for debts.

If thou hast nothing to pay, why should he take away thy bed from under thee?
PROVERBS 22:26–27

COMFORT

WE NEED NEVER SHOUT
ACROSS THE SPACES
TO AN ABSENT GOD.
HE IS NEARER THAN
OUR OWN SOUL,
CLOSER THAN OUR
MOST SECRET THOUGHTS.
A. W. Tozer

Come unto me, all ye that labour and are heavy laden, and I will give you rest.   MATTHEW 11:28

And it shall come to pass in the day that the LORD shall give thee rest from thy sorrow, and from thy fear, and from the hard bondage wherein thou wast made to serve.   ISAIAH 14:3

Yea, though I walk through the valley of the shadow of death, I will fear no evil: for thou art with me; thy rod and thy staff they comfort me.   PSALM 23:4

And God shall wipe away all tears from their eyes; and there shall be no more death, neither sorrow, nor crying, neither shall there be any more pain: for the former things are passed away.   REVELATION 21:4

For the Lord himself shall descend from heaven with a shout, with the voice of the archangel, and with the trump of God: and the dead in Christ shall rise first:

Then we which are alive and remain shall be caught up together with them in the clouds, to meet the Lord in the air: and so shall we ever be with the Lord.

Wherefore comfort one another with these words.   1 THESSALONIANS 4:16–18

He hath put forth his hands against such as be at peace with him: he hath broken his covenant.
                                    PSALM 55:20

God is our refuge and strength, a very present help in trouble.

Therefore will not we fear, though the earth be removed, and though the mountains be carried into the midst of the sea;

Though the waters thereof roar and be troubled, though the mountains shake with the swelling thereof.   PSALM 46:1–3

Comfort ye, comfort ye my people, saith your God.

ISAIAH 40:1

And I will pray the Father, and he shall give you another Comforter, that he may abide with you for ever.

JOHN 14:16

The Spirit of the Lord GOD is upon me; because the LORD hath anointed me to preach good tidings unto the meek; he hath sent me to bind up the brokenhearted, to proclaim liberty to the captives, and the opening of the prison to them that are bound;

To proclaim the acceptable year of the LORD, and the day of vengeance of our God; to comfort all that mourn.

ISAIAH 61:1–2

Yet man is born unto trouble, as the sparks fly upward.

I would seek unto God, and unto God would I commit my cause.

JOB 5:7–8

CASTING ALL YOUR CARE UPON HIM; FOR HE CARETH FOR YOU.

1 Peter 5:7

Blessed are they that mourn: for they shall be comforted.

MATTHEW 5:4

The Lord GOD will wipe away tears from off all faces.

ISAIAH 25:8

And, lo, I am with you alway, even unto the end of the world.   MATTHEW 28:20

I WILL NOT LEAVE
YOU COMFORTLESS:
I WILL COME TO YOU.
John 14:18

Blessed be God, even the Father of our Lord Jesus Christ, the Father of mercies, and the God of all comfort;

Who comforteth us in all our tribulation, that we may be able to comfort them which are in any trouble, by the comfort wherewith we ourselves are comforted of God.

For as the sufferings of Christ abound in us, so our consolation also aboundeth by Christ.
                                    2 CORINTHIANS 1:3–5

CONVERSATION

SPEAK SOFTLY.
IT IS FAR BETTER TO
RULE BY LOVE THAN FEAR.
SPEAK SOFTLY.
LET NO HARSH WORDS
MAR THE GOOD
WE MAY DO HERE.

Isaac Watts

In the multitude of words there wanteth not sin: but he that refraineth his lips is wise. PROVERBS 10:19

For though I would desire to glory, I shall not be a fool; for I will say the truth: but now I forbear, lest any man should think of me above that which he seeth me to be, or that he heareth of me.

2 CORINTHIANS 12:6

A fool uttereth all his mind: but a wise man keepeth it in till afterwards.   PROVERBS 29:11

But now ye also put off all these; anger, wrath, malice, blasphemy, filthy communication out of your mouth.   COLOSSIANS 3:8

A word fitly spoken is like apples of gold in pictures of silver.   PROVERBS 25:11

I said, I will take heed to my ways, that I sin not with my tongue: I will keep my mouth with a bridle, while the wicked is before me.   PSALM 39:1

A soft answer turneth away wrath: but grievous words stir up anger.   PROVERBS 15:1

A talebearer revealeth secrets: but he that is of a faithful spirit concealeth the matter.   PROVERBS 11:13

Set a watch, O LORD, before my mouth; keep the door of my lips.   PSALM 141:3

There is that speaketh like the piercings of a sword: but the tongue of the wise is health.

PROVERBS 12:18

If any man offend not in word, the same is a perfect man, and able also to bridle the whole body.

JAMES 3:2

A time to rend, and a time to sew; a time to keep
silence, and a time to speak.　　ECCLESIASTES 3:7

> A MAN HATH JOY
> BY THE ANSWER
> OF HIS MOUTH:
> AND A WORD SPOKEN
> IN DUE SEASON,
> HOW GOOD IS IT!
> *Proverbs 15:23*

The heart of the righteous studieth to answer: but
the mouth of the wicked poureth out evil things.
　　　　　　　　　　　　　　　PROVERBS 15:28

Let your speech be alway with grace, seasoned with
salt, that ye may know how ye ought to answer
every man.　　　　　　　　　COLOSSIANS 4:6

HE THAT WON'T BE COUNSELLED CAN'T BE HELPED.
Benjamin Franklin

As every man hath received the gift, even so minister the same one to another, as good stewards of the manifold grace of God.   1 PETER 4:10

Brethren, if a man be overtaken in a fault, ye which are spiritual, restore such an one in the spirit of meekness; considering thyself, lest thou also be tempted.
GALATIANS 6:1

And all thy children shall be taught of the LORD; and great shall be the peace of thy children.
ISAIAH 54:13

Now no chastening for the present seemeth to be joyous, but grievous: nevertheless afterward it yieldeth the peaceable fruit of righteousness unto them which are exercised thereby.　　　HEBREWS 12:11

For unto us a child is born, unto us a son is given: and the government shall be upon his shoulder: and his name shall be called Wonderful, Counsellor, The mighty God, The everlasting Father, The Prince of Peace.　　　ISAIAH 9:6

Hear counsel, and receive instruction, that thou mayest be wise in thy latter end.　　　PROVERBS 19:20

Howbeit when he, the Spirit of truth, is come, he will guide you into all truth: for he shall not speak of himself; but whatsoever he shall hear, that shall he speak: and he will shew you things to come.　　　JOHN 16:13

Give instruction to a wise man, and he will be yet wiser: teach a just man, and he will increase in learning.　　　PROVERBS 9:9

The way of a fool is right in his own eyes: but he that hearkeneth unto counsel is wise.　　　PROVERBS 12:15

Ointment and perfume rejoice the heart: so doth the sweetness of a man's friend by hearty counsel.　　　PROVERBS 27:9

Without counsel purposes are disappointed: but in the multitude of counsellors they are established.

PROVERBS 15:22

WHERE NO COUNSEL IS,
THE PEOPLE FALL:
BUT IN THE MULTITUDE
OF COUNSELLORS
THERE IS SAFETY.
Proverbs 11:14

A wise man will hear, and will increase learning; and a man of understanding shall attain unto wise counsels.

PROVERBS 1:5

COURAGE

**COURAGE IS
THE FIRST OF
HUMAN QUALITIES BECAUSE
IT IS THE QUALITY WHICH
GUARANTEES ALL OTHERS.**
Winston Churchill

Wait on the LORD: be of good courage, and he shall strengthen thine heart: wait, I say, on the LORD.
PSALM 27:14

For God hath not given us the spirit of fear; but of power, and of love, and of a sound mind.
2 TIMOTHY 1:7

So that we may boldly say, The Lord is my helper, and I will not fear what man shall do unto me.
HEBREWS 13:6

Only let your conversation be as it becometh the gospel of Christ: that whether I come and see you, or else be absent, I may hear of your affairs, that ye stand fast in one spirit, with one mind striving together for the faith of the gospel;

And in nothing terrified by your adversaries: which is to them an evident token of perdition, but to you of salvation, and that of God.

PHILIPPIANS 1:27–28

And now, little children, abide in him; that, when he shall appear, we may have confidence, and not be ashamed before him at his coming.   1 JOHN 2:28

In the fear of the LORD is strong confidence: and his children shall have a place of refuge.

PROVERBS 14:26

WATCH YE,
STAND FAST IN THE FAITH,
QUIT YOU LIKE MEN,
BE STRONG.
1 Corinthians 16:13

And thou, son of man, be not afraid of them, neither be afraid of their words, though briers and thorns be with thee, and thou dost dwell among scorpions: be not afraid of their words, nor be dismayed at their looks, though they be a rebellious house.   EZEKIEL 2:6

The wicked flee when no man pursueth: but the righteous are bold as a lion.   PROVERBS 28:1

Having therefore, brethren, boldness to enter into the holiest by the blood of Jesus.   HEBREWS 10:19

Be of good courage, and he shall strengthen your heart, all ye that hope in the LORD.   PSALM 31:24

In whom we have boldness and access with confidence by the faith of him.   EPHESIANS 3:12

For the LORD shall be thy confidence, and shall keep thy foot from being taken.   PROVERBS 3:26

STEER CLEAR OF
ANYONE WHO VALUES
CLEVERNESS ABOVE
DEPENDABILITY,
EXPEDIENCE ABOVE
INTEGRITY,
AND CHARM ABOVE
CHARACTER.

William Arthur Ward

And the Lord said, Who then is that faithful and wise steward, whom his lord shall make ruler over his household, to give them their portion of meat in due season? LUKE 12:42

And he spake a parable unto them to this end, that men ought always to pray, and not to faint.

LUKE 18:1

But he that shall endure unto the end, the same shall be saved. MATTHEW 24:13

Be not carried about with divers and strange doctrines. For it is a good thing that the heart be established with grace; not with meats, which have not profited them that have been occupied therein. HEBREWS 13:9

And ye have forgotten the exhortation which speaketh unto you as unto children, My son, despise not thou the chastening of the Lord, nor faint when thou art rebuked of him. HEBREWS 12:5

TEACH ME, O LORD,
THE WAY OF THY STATUTES;
AND I SHALL KEEP IT
UNTO THE END.
Psalm 119:33

Let a man so account of us, as of the ministers of Christ, and stewards of the mysteries of God.

Moreover it is required in stewards, that a man be found faithful. 1 CORINTHIANS 4:1–2

Wherefore we labour, that, whether present or absent, we may be accepted of him.
2 CORINTHIANS 5:9

He shall not be afraid of evil tidings: his heart is fixed, trusting in the LORD. PSALM 112:7

Let your loins be girded about, and your lights burning;

And ye yourselves like unto men that wait for their lord, when he will return from the wedding; that when he cometh and knocketh, they may open unto him immediately. LUKE 12:35–36

For if any be a hearer of the word, and not a doer, he is like unto a man beholding his natural face in a glass:

For he beholdeth himself, and goeth his way, and straightway forgetteth what manner of man he was.

But whoso looketh into the perfect law of liberty, and continueth therein, he being not a forgetful hearer, but a doer of the work, this man shall be blessed in his deed. JAMES 1:23–25

My heart is fixed, O God, my heart is fixed: I will sing and give praise. PSALM 57:7

DILIGENCE

NEVER LEAVE THAT
TILL TOMORROW WHICH
YOU CAN DO TODAY.

Benjamin Franklin

Labour not for the meat which perisheth, but for that meat which endureth unto everlasting life, which the Son of man shall give unto you: for him hath God the Father sealed. JOHN 6:27

Whatsoever is commanded by the God of heaven, let it be diligently done for the house of the God of heaven: for why should there be wrath against the realm of the king and his sons? EZRA 7:23

But ye, brethren, be not weary in well doing.
2 THESSALONIANS 3:13

Wherefore the rather, brethren, give diligence to make your calling and election sure: for if ye do these things, ye shall never fall:

For so an entrance shall be ministered unto you abundantly into the everlasting kingdom of our Lord and Saviour Jesus Christ.   2 PETER 1:10–11

Behold that which I have seen: it is good and comely for one to eat and to drink, and to enjoy the good of all his labour that he taketh under the sun all the days of his life, which God giveth him: for it is his portion.

Every man also to whom God hath given riches and wealth, and hath given him power to eat thereof, and to take his portion, and to rejoice in his labour; this is the gift of God.   ECCLESIASTES 5:18–19

I MUST WORK
THE WORKS OF
HIM THAT SENT ME,
WHILE IT IS DAY:
THE NIGHT COMETH,
WHEN NO MAN
CAN WORK.
John 9:4

Or he that exhorteth, on exhortation: he that giveth, let him do it with simplicity; he that ruleth, with diligence; he that sheweth mercy, with cheerfulness.

ROMANS 12:8

The thoughts of the diligent tend only to plenteousness; but of every one that is hasty only to want.

PROVERBS 21:5

Wherefore, beloved, seeing that ye look for such things, be diligent that ye may be found of him in peace, without spot, and blameless.   2 PETER 3:14

And let us not be weary in well doing: for in due season we shall reap, if we faint not.

GALATIANS 6:9

Therefore, my beloved brethren, be ye stedfast, unmoveable, always abounding in the work of the Lord, forasmuch as ye know that your labour is not in vain in the Lord.   1 CORINTHIANS 15:58

And beside this, giving all diligence, add to your faith virtue; and to virtue knowledge.   2 PETER 1:5

A FAMILY IS
A PLACE WHERE
PRINCIPLES ARE HAMMERED
AND HONED ON THE ANVIL
OF EVERYDAY LIVING.

Charles Swindoll

One that ruleth well his own house, having his children in subjection with all gravity;
(For if a man know not how to rule his own house, how shall he take care of the church of God?)
1 TIMOTHY 3:4–5

Withhold not correction from the child: for if thou beatest him with the rod, he shall not die.
Thou shalt beat him with the rod, and shalt deliver his soul from hell.   PROVERBS 23:13–14

Foolishness is bound in the heart of a child; but the rod of correction shall drive it far from him.

PROVERBS 22:15

HE THAT SPARETH HIS ROD HATETH HIS SON: BUT HE THAT LOVETH HIM CHASTENETH HIM BETIMES.

Proverbs 13:24

Correct thy son, and he shall give thee rest; yea, he shall give delight unto thy soul.   PROVERBS 29:17

Now, lo, if he beget a son, that seeth all his father's sins which he hath done, and considereth, and doeth not such like,

That hath not eaten upon the mountains, neither hath lifted up his eyes to the idols of the house of Israel, hath not defiled his neighbour's wife,

Neither hath oppressed any, hath not withholden the pledge, neither hath spoiled by violence, but hath given his bread to the hungry, and hath covered the naked with a garment,

That hath taken off his hand from the poor, that hath not received usury nor increase, hath executed my judgments, hath walked in my statutes; he shall not die for the iniquity of his father, he shall surely live.   EZEKIEL 18:14–17

And, ye fathers, provoke not your children to wrath:
but bring them up in the nurture and admonition of
the Lord.   EPHESIANS 6:4

Chasten thy son while there is hope, and let not thy
soul spare for his crying.   PROVERBS 19:18

Even a child is known by his doings, whether his
work be pure, and whether it be right.
                                        PROVERBS 20:11

FATHERS,
PROVOKE NOT YOUR
CHILDREN TO ANGER,
LEST THEY BE
DISCOURAGED.
Colossians 3:21

DISCIPLINE, GOD'S

THE REASON WE ARE ALL BEING DISCIPLINED IS THAT WE WILL KNOW GOD IS REAL.

Oswald Chambers

Blessed is the man whom thou chastenest, O LORD, and teachest him out of thy law.　　PSALM 94:12

For whom the Lord loveth he chasteneth, and scourgeth every son whom he receiveth.　HEBREWS 12:6

Behold, happy is the man whom God correcteth: therefore despise not thou the chastening of the Almighty:

For he maketh sore, and bindeth up: he woundeth, and his hands make whole.　　JOB 5:17–18

If ye endure chastening, God dealeth with you as with sons; for what son is he whom the father chasteneth not?   HEBREWS 12:7

Blessed is the man whom thou chastenest, O LORD, and teachest him out of thy law;
    That thou mayest give him rest from the days of adversity, until the pit be digged for the wicked.
                                PSALM 94:12–13

For the commandment is a lamp; and the law is light; and reproofs of instruction are the way of life.
                                PROVERBS 6:23

For whom the LORD loveth he correcteth; even as a father the son in whom he delighteth.
                                PROVERBS 3:12

Now no chastening for the present seemeth to be joyous, but grievous: nevertheless afterward it yieldeth the peaceable fruit of righteousness unto them which are exercised thereby.   HEBREWS 12:11

IF DOING A GOOD ACT
IN PUBLIC WILL
EXCITE OTHERS
TO DO MORE GOOD,
THEN ... 'LET YOUR LIGHT
SHINE TO ALL ...'
MISS NO OPPORTUNITY
TO DO GOOD.

John Wesley

And why call ye me, Lord, Lord, and do not the things which I say?   LUKE 6:46

Now therefore, if ye will obey my voice indeed, and keep my covenant, then ye shall be a peculiar treasure unto me above all people: for all the earth is mine.
EXODUS 19:5

Thou shalt keep therefore his statutes, and his commandments, which I command thee this day, that it may go well with thee, and with thy children after thee, and that thou mayest prolong thy days upon the earth, which the LORD thy God giveth thee, for ever.   DEUTERONOMY 4:40

When a man's ways please the LORD, he maketh even his enemies to be at peace with him.
                                        PROVERBS 16:7

Save when there shall be no poor among you; for the LORD shall greatly bless thee in the land which the LORD thy God giveth thee for an inheritance to possess it:
 Only if thou carefully hearken unto the voice of the LORD thy God, to observe to do all these commandments which I command thee this day.
                              DEUTERONOMY 15:4–5

See, I have set before thee this day life and good, and death and evil;
 In that I command thee this day to love the LORD thy God, to walk in his ways, and to keep his commandments and his statutes and his judgments, that thou mayest live and multiply: and the LORD thy God shall bless thee in the land whither thou goest to possess it.   DEUTERONOMY 30:15–16

If ye be willing and obedient, ye shall eat the good of the land.   ISAIAH 1:19

And he sought God in the days of Zechariah, who had understanding in the visions of God: and as long as he sought the LORD, God made him to prosper.

2 CHRONICLES 26:5

If they obey and serve him, they shall spend their days in prosperity, and their years in pleasures.

JOB 36:11

AND SHEWING MERCY UNTO THOUSANDS OF THEM THAT LOVE ME, AND KEEP MY COMMANDMENTS.
Exodus 20:6

Observe and hear all these words which I command thee, that it may go well with thee, and with thy children after thee for ever, when thou doest that which is good and right in the sight of the LORD thy God.

DEUTERONOMY 12:28

And ye shall be hated of all men for my name's sake: but he that endureth to the end shall be saved.

MATTHEW 10:22

THE WORLD IS IN DIRE NEED OF ENCOURAGERS.

G. E. Dean

I can do all things through Christ which strengtheneth me.   PHILIPPIANS 4:13

Therefore, brethren, stand fast, and hold the tradi-
tions which ye have been taught, whether by word, or
our epistle.

Now our Lord Jesus Christ himself, and God,
even our Father, which hath loved us, and hath given
us everlasting consolation and good hope through
grace,

Comfort your hearts, and stablish you in every
good word and work.   2 THESSALONIANS 2:15–17

He giveth power to the faint; and to them that have no might he increaseth strength.   ISAIAH 40:29

And when they bring you unto the synagogues, and unto magistrates, and powers, take ye no thought how or what thing ye shall answer, or what ye shall say:

For the Holy Ghost shall teach you in the same hour what ye ought to say.   LUKE 12:11–12

All scripture is given by inspiration of God, and is profitable for doctrine, for reproof, for correction, for instruction in righteousness.   2 TIMOTHY 3:16

Brethren, if any of you do err from the truth, and one convert him;

Let him know, that he which converteth the sinner from the error of his way shall save a soul from death, and shall hide a multitude of sins.

JAMES 5:19–20

And whether we be afflicted, it is for your consolation and salvation, which is effectual in the enduring of the same sufferings which we also suffer: or whether we be comforted, it is for your consolation and salvation.   2 CORINTHIANS 1:6

Wherefore comfort yourselves together, and edify one another, even as also ye do.

1 THESSALONIANS 5:11

Look not every man on his own things, but every man also on the things of others.   PHILIPPIANS 2:4

BEAR YE ONE
ANOTHER'S BURDENS,
AND SO FULFIL
THE LAW OF CHRIST.
Galatians 6:2

Ye are witnesses, and God also, how holily and justly and unblameably we behaved ourselves among you that believe:

As ye know how we exhorted and comforted and charged every one of you, as a father doth his children,

That ye would walk worthy of God, who hath called you unto his kingdom and glory.

For this cause also thank we God without ceasing, because, when ye received the word of God which ye heard of us, ye received it not as the word of men, but as it is in truth, the word of God, which effectually worketh also in you that believe.

1 THESSALONIANS 2:10–13

ENEMIES

IF I MAKE MY ENEMY MY FRIEND,
HAVE I NOT
DESTROYED MY ENEMIES?
Abraham Lincoln

Bless them which persecute you: bless, and curse not.
ROMANS 12:14

When a man's ways please the LORD, he maketh even his enemies to be at peace with him.
PROVERBS 16:7

Therefore if thine enemy hunger, feed him; if he thirst, give him drink: for in so doing thou shalt heap coals of fire on his head.
Be not overcome of evil, but overcome evil with good.
ROMANS 12:20–21

For the Lord your God is he that goeth with you, to fight for you against your enemies, to save you.

DEUTERONOMY 20:4

Thou preparest a table before me in the presence of mine enemies: thou anointest my head with oil; my cup runneth over.

PSALM 23:5

SO THAT WE MAY
BOLDLY SAY,
THE LORD IS MY HELPER,
AND I WILL NOT FEAR
WHAT MAN SHALL DO
UNTO ME.
Hebrews 13:6

That he would grant unto us, that we, being delivered out of the hand of our enemies, might serve him without fear.

LUKE 1:74

Though I walk in the midst of trouble, thou wilt revive me: thou shalt stretch forth thine hand against the wrath of mine enemies, and thy right hand shall save me.

PSALM 138:7

Agree with thine adversary quickly, whiles thou art in the way with him; lest at any time the adversary deliver thee to the judge, and the judge deliver thee to the officer, and thou be cast into prison.

MATTHEW 5:25

For in the time of trouble he shall hide me in his pavilion: in the secret of his tabernacle shall he hide me; he shall set me up upon a rock.

And now shall mine head be lifted up above mine enemies round about me: therefore will I offer in his tabernacle sacrifices of joy; I will sing, yea, I will sing praises unto the LORD.

PSALM 27:5–6

And the LORD shall help them, and deliver them: he shall deliver them from the wicked, and save them, because they trust in him.   PSALM 37:40

If thine enemy be hungry, give him bread to eat; and if he be thirsty, give him water to drink:

For thou shalt heap coals of fire upon his head, and the LORD shall reward thee.

PROVERBS 25:21–22

HE IS NO FOOL WHO
GIVES WHAT
HE CANNOT KEEP
TO GAIN WHAT
HE CANNOT LOSE.
Jim Elliot

Nevertheless we, according to his promise, look for new heavens and a new earth, wherein dwelleth righteousness.   2 PETER 3:13

And I give unto them eternal life; and they shall never perish, neither shall any man pluck them out of my hand.   JOHN 10:28

He that loveth his life shall lose it; and he that hateth his life in this world shall keep it unto life eternal.   JOHN 12:25

For the wages of sin is death; but the gift of God is eternal life through Jesus Christ our Lord.

ROMANS 6:23

Behold, I shew you a mystery; We shall not all sleep, but we shall all be changed,

In a moment, in the twinkling of an eye, at the last trump: for the trumpet shall sound, and the dead shall be raised incorruptible, and we shall be changed.

For this corruptible must put on incorruption, and this mortal must put on immortality.

So when this corruptible shall have put on incorruption, and this mortal shall have put on immortality, then shall be brought to pass the saying that is written, Death is swallowed up in victory.

1 CORINTHIANS 15:51–54

And this is the record, that God hath given to us eternal life, and this life is in his Son.   1 JOHN 5:11

Jesus said unto her, I am the resurrection, and the life: he that believeth in me, though he were dead, yet shall he live:

And whosoever liveth and believeth in me shall never die. Believest thou this?   JOHN 11:25–26

God. . .will render to every man according to his deeds: To them who by patient continuance in well doing seek for glory and honour and immortality, eternal life.

ROMANS 2:5–7

Labour not for the meat which perisheth, but for that meat which endureth unto everlasting life, which the Son of man shall give unto you: for him hath God the Father sealed.   JOHN 6:27

AND WHEN
THE CHIEF SHEPHERD
SHALL APPEAR,
YE SHALL RECEIVE
A CROWN OF GLORY
THAT FADETH NOT AWAY.
1 Peter 5:4

And many of them that sleep in the dust of the earth shall awake, some to everlasting life, and some to shame and everlasting contempt.   DANIEL 12:2

Henceforth there is laid up for me a crown of right-eousness, which the Lord, the righteous judge, shall give me at that day: and not to me only, but unto all them also that love his appearing.   2 TIMOTHY 4:8

For we know that if our earthly house of this taber-nacle were dissolved, we have a building of God, an house not made with hands, eternal in the heavens.
2 CORINTHIANS 5:1

But if the Spirit of him that raised up Jesus from the dead dwell in you, he that raised up Christ from the dead shall also quicken your mortal bodies by his Spirit that dwelleth in you.   ROMANS 8:11

And there shall be no night there; and they need no candle, neither light of the sun; for the Lord God giveth them light: and they shall reign for ever and ever.　　　　　　　　　　　　　　　REVELATION 22:5

And the world passeth away, and the lust thereof: but he that doeth the will of God abideth for ever.
　　　　　　　　　　　　　　　　　　　　1 JOHN 2:17

Verily, verily, I say unto you, He that heareth my word, and believeth on him that sent me, hath everlasting life, and shall not come into condemnation; but is passed from death unto life.　　　　JOHN 5:24

Blessed be the God and Father of our Lord Jesus Christ, which according to his abundant mercy hath begotten us again unto a lively hope by the resurrection of Jesus Christ from the dead,
　　To an inheritance incorruptible, and undefiled, and that fadeth not away, reserved in heaven for you,
　　Who are kept by the power of God through faith unto salvation ready to be revealed in the last time.
　　　　　　　　　　　　　　　　　　　1 PETER 1:3–5

In my Father's house are many mansions: if it were not so, I would have told you. I go to prepare a place for you.
　　And if I go and prepare a place for you, I will come again, and receive you unto myself; that where I am, there ye may be also.　　　　JOHN 14:2–3

He that soweth to the Spirit shall of the Spirit reap life everlasting. GALATIANS 6:8

> SEARCH THE SCRIPTURES;
> FOR IN THEM YE THINK YE
> HAVE ETERNAL LIFE:
> AND THEY ARE THEY
> WHICH TESTIFY OF ME.
> *John 5:39*

Therefore are they before the throne of God, and serve him day and night in his temple: and he that sitteth on the throne shall dwell among them.

They shall hunger no more, neither thirst any more; neither shall the sun light on them, nor any heat.

For the Lamb which is in the midst of the throne shall feed them, and shall lead them unto living fountains of waters: and God shall wipe away all tears from their eyes. REVELATION 7:15–17

FAITH IS NOT
THE ABSENCE OF QUESTIONING;
IT IS THE PRESENCE OF
ACTION IN THE MIDST OF
THOSE QUESTIONS.

Woodrow Kroll

Now faith is the substance of things hoped for, the evidence of things not seen. HEBREWS 11:1

That Christ may dwell in your hearts by faith; that ye, being rooted and grounded in love,
    May be able to comprehend with all saints what is the breadth, and length, and depth, and height;
    And to know the love of Christ, which passeth knowledge, that ye might be filled with all the fulness of God. EPHESIANS 3:17–19

Jesus said unto him, If thou canst believe, all things are possible to him that believeth.   MARK 9:23

It is written in the prophets, And they shall be all taught of God. Every man therefore that hath heard, and hath learned of the Father, cometh unto me.
JOHN 6:45

That your faith should not stand in the wisdom of men, but in the power of God.
1 CORINTHIANS 2:5

Ask in faith, nothing wavering. For he that wavereth is like a wave of the sea driven with the wind and tossed.   JAMES 1:6

And the Lord said, If ye had faith as a grain of mustard seed, ye might say unto this sycamine tree, Be thou plucked up by the root, and be thou planted in the sea; and it should obey you.   LUKE 17:6

For we walk by faith, not by sight.
2 CORINTHIANS 5:7

Whom having not seen, ye love; in whom, though now ye see him not, yet believing, ye rejoice with joy unspeakable and full of glory.   1 PETER 1:8

As soon as Jesus heard the word that was spoken, he saith unto the ruler of the synagogue, Be not afraid, only believe.   MARK 5:36

For ye are all the children of God by faith in Christ
Jesus.   GALATIANS 3:26

AND HE SAID
TO THE WOMAN,
THY FAITH HATH SAVED
THEE; GO IN PEACE.
Luke 7:50

But as many as received him, to them gave he power
to become the sons of God, even to them that
believe on his name.   JOHN 1:12

He that believeth and is baptized shall be saved; but
he that believeth not shall be damned.
                                        MARK 16:16

That if thou shalt confess with thy mouth the Lord
Jesus, and shalt believe in thine heart that God hath
raised him from the dead, thou shalt be saved.
                                        ROMANS 10:9

Let us draw near with a true heart in full assurance
of faith, having our hearts sprinkled from an evil
conscience, and our bodies washed with pure water.
                                        HEBREWS 10:22

He that believeth on the Son of God hath the witness in himself: he that believeth not God hath
made him a liar; because he believeth not the record
that God gave of his Son.   1 JOHN 5:10

Watch ye, stand fast in the faith, quit you like men, be strong. 1 CORINTHIANS 16:13

Behold, I stand at the door, and knock: if any man hear my voice, and open the door, I will come in to him, and will sup with him, and he with me.
REVELATION 3:20

Jesus saith unto her, Said I not unto thee, that, if thou wouldest believe, thou shouldest see the glory of God? JOHN 11:40

The life which I now live in the flesh I live by the faith of the Son of God, who loved me, and gave himself for me. GALATIANS 2:20

JESUS ANSWERED AND
SAID UNTO THEM,
THIS IS THE WORK OF GOD,
THAT YE BELIEVE ON HIM
WHOM HE HATH SENT.
John 6:29

And Jesus answering saith unto them, Have faith in God.
For verily I say unto you, That whosoever shall say unto this mountain, Be thou removed, and be thou cast into the sea; and shall not doubt in his heart, but shall believe that those things which he saith shall come to pass; he shall have whatsoever he saith. MARK 11:22–23

As ye have therefore received Christ Jesus the Lord, so walk ye in him. COLOSSIANS 2:6–7

For by grace are ye saved through faith; and that not of yourselves: it is the gift of God. EPHESIANS 2:8

Jesus saith unto him, Thomas, because thou hast seen me, thou hast believed: blessed are they that have not seen, and yet have believed. JOHN 20:29

But without faith it is impossible to please him: for he that cometh to God must believe that he is, and that he is a rewarder of them that diligently seek him. HEBREWS 11:6

FAITHFULNESS OF GOD

YOUR HEAVENLY FATHER
IS TOO GOOD TO BE
UNKIND AND TOO WISE TO
MAKE MISTAKES.
Charles H. Spurgeon

Be thou faithful unto death, and I will give thee a crown of life. REVELATION 2:10

God is not a man, that he should lie; neither the son of man, that he should repent: hath he said, and shall he not do it? Or hath he spoken, and shall he not make it good? NUMBERS 23:19

O love the LORD, all ye his saints: for the LORD preserveth the faithful, and plentifully rewardeth the proud doer. PSALM 31:23

Blessed be the LORD, that hath given rest unto his people Israel, according to all that he promised: there hath not failed one word of all his good promise, which he promised by the hand of Moses his servant. 1 KINGS 8:56

Know therefore that the LORD thy God, he is God, the faithful God, which keepeth covenant and mercy with them that love him and keep his commandments to a thousand generations.

DEUTERONOMY 7:9

If we believe not, yet he abideth faithful: he cannot deny himself. 2 TIMOTHY 2:13

And we know that all things work together for good to them that love God, to them who are the called according to his purpose. ROMANS 8:28

And the heavens shall praise thy wonders, O LORD: thy faithfulness also in the congregation of the saints. PSALM 89:5

A faithful man shall abound with blessings: but he that maketh haste to be rich shall not be innocent.

PROVERBS 28:20

Therefore thus saith the Lord GOD, Behold, I lay in Zion for a foundation a stone, a tried stone, a precious corner stone, a sure foundation: he that believeth shall not make haste. ISAIAH 28:16

IN HOPE OF ETERNAL LIFE,
WHICH GOD,
THAT CANNOT LIE,
PROMISED BEFORE THE
WORLD BEGAN.
Titus 1:2

Who then is a faithful and wise servant, whom his lord hath made ruler over his household, to give them meat in due season?

Blessed is that servant, whom his lord when he cometh shall find so doing.

Verily I say unto you, That he shall make him ruler over all his goods.   MATTHEW 24:45–47

THE BUSINESS OF OUR LIVES IS NOT TO PLEASE OURSELVES BUT TO PLEASE GOD.

Matthew Henry

And fear not them which kill the body, but are not able to kill the soul: but rather fear him which is able to destroy both soul and body in hell.

MATTHEW 10:28

Moreover thou shalt provide out of all the people able men, such as fear God, men of truth, hating covetousness; and place such over them, to be rulers of thousands, and rulers of hundreds, rulers of fifties, and rulers of tens.　　EXODUS 18:21

A wise man feareth, and departeth from evil: but the fool rageth, and is confident.　PROVERBS 14:16

The fear of the LORD is the beginning of knowledge: but fools despise wisdom and instruction.

PROVERBS 1:7

Saying with a loud voice, Fear God, and give glory to him; for the hour of his judgment is come: and worship him that made heaven, and earth, and the sea, and the fountains of waters.   REVELATION 14:7

O that there were such an heart in them, that they would fear me, and keep all my commandments always, that it might be well with them, and with their children for ever!   DEUTERONOMY 5:29

The angel of the LORD encampeth round about them that fear him, and delivereth them.

PSALM 34:7

Only fear the LORD, and serve him in truth with all your heart: for consider how great things he hath done for you.   1 SAMUEL 12:24

Thou believest that there is one God; thou doest well: the devils also believe, and tremble.

JAMES 2:19

Wherefore we receiving a kingdom which cannot be moved, let us have grace, whereby we may serve God acceptably with reverence and godly fear:
    For our God is a consuming fire.

HEBREWS 12:28–29

Men do therefore fear him: he respecteth not any that are wise of heart. JOB 37:24

Wherefore, my beloved, as ye have always obeyed, not as in my presence only, but now much more in my absence, work out your own salvation with fear and trembling. PHILIPPIANS 2:12

> SERVE THE LORD
> WITH FEAR,
> AND REJOICE
> WITH TREMBLING.
> *Psalm 2:11*

Having therefore these promises, dearly beloved, let us cleanse ourselves from all filthiness of the flesh and spirit, perfecting holiness in the fear of God.
2 CORINTHIANS 7:1

The fear of the LORD is to hate evil: pride, and arrogancy, and the evil way, and the froward mouth, do I hate. PROVERBS 8:13

Let us hear the conclusion of the whole matter: Fear God, and keep his commandments: for this is the whole duty of man. ECCLESIASTES 12:13

Then they that feared the LORD spake often one to another: and the LORD hearkened, and heard it, and a book of remembrance was written before him for them that feared the LORD, and that thought upon his name. MALACHI 3:16

Fear ye not me? saith the LORD: will ye not tremble at my presence, which have placed the sand for the bound of the sea by a perpetual decree, that it cannot pass it: and though the waves thereof toss themselves, yet can they not prevail; though they roar, yet can they not pass over it?   JEREMIAH 5:22

HE WILL FULFIL THE DESIRE
OF THEM THAT FEAR HIM:
HE ALSO WILL HEAR THEIR
CRY, AND WILL SAVE THEM.
Psalm 145:19

The secret of the LORD is with them that fear him; and he will shew them his covenant.   PSALM 25:14

FORGIVENESS IS
THE OIL OF RELATIONSHIPS.
Josh McDowell

For if ye forgive men their trespasses, your heavenly Father will also forgive you:

But if ye forgive not men their trespasses, neither will your Father forgive your trespasses.

MATTHEW 6:14–15

The discretion of a man deferreth his anger; and it is his glory to pass over a transgression.

PROVERBS 19:11

Not rendering evil for evil, or railing for railing: but contrariwise blessing; knowing that ye are thereunto called, that ye should inherit a blessing.

1 PETER 3:9

But I say unto you, That ye resist not evil: but whosoever shall smite thee on thy right cheek, turn to him the other also.

And if any man will sue thee at the law, and take away thy coat, let him have thy cloke also.

And whosoever shall compel thee to go a mile, go with him twain. MATTHEW 5:39–41

And be ye kind one to another, tenderhearted, forgiving one another, even as God for Christ's sake hath forgiven you. EPHESIANS 4:32

Take heed to yourselves: If thy brother trespass against thee, rebuke him; and if he repent, forgive him.

And if he trespass against thee seven times in a day, and seven times in a day turn again to thee, saying, I repent; thou shalt forgive him. LUKE 17:3–4

Then came Peter to him, and said, Lord, how oft shall my brother sin against me, and I forgive him? till seven times?

Jesus saith unto him, I say not unto thee, Until seven times: but, Until seventy times seven.
MATTHEW 18:21–22

And when ye stand praying, forgive, if ye have ought against any: that your Father also which is in heaven may forgive you your trespasses.

But if ye do not forgive, neither will your Father which is in heaven forgive your trespasses.
MARK 11:25–26

AND FORGIVE US OUR SINS;
FOR WE ALSO FORGIVE
EVERY ONE THAT IS
INDEBTED TO US.
AND LEAD US NOT INTO
TEMPTATION; BUT
DELIVER US FROM EVIL.
Luke 11:4

Forbearing one another, and forgiving one another, if any man have a quarrel against any: even as Christ forgave you, so also do ye.   COLOSSIANS 3:13

GIVE WHAT YOU HAVE.
TO SOMEONE,
IT MAY BE BETTER THAN
YOU DARE TO THINK.
Henry Wadsworth Longfellow

Therefore when thou doest thine alms, do not sound a trumpet before thee, as the hypocrites do in the synagogues and in the streets, that they may have glory of men. Verily I say unto you, They have their reward.

But when thou doest alms, let not thy left hand know what thy right hand doeth:

That thine alms may be in secret: and thy Father which seeth in secret himself shall reward thee openly.　　　　　　　　　MATTHEW 6:2–4

And if thy brother be waxen poor, and fallen in decay with thee; then thou shalt relieve him: yea, though he be a stranger, or a sojourner; that he may live with thee.   LEVITICUS 25:35

If any man or woman that believeth have widows, let them relieve them, and let not the church be charged; that it may relieve them that are widows indeed.   1 TIMOTHY 5:16

For the poor shall never cease out of the land: therefore I command thee, saying, Thou shalt open thine hand wide unto thy brother, to thy poor, and to thy needy, in thy land.   DEUTERONOMY 15:11

If a brother or sister be naked, and destitute of daily food,
    And one of you say unto them, Depart in peace, be ye warmed and filled; notwithstanding ye give them not those things which are needful to the body; what doth it profit?   JAMES 2:15–16

Is it not to deal thy bread to the hungry, and that thou bring the poor that are cast out to thy house? when thou seest the naked, that thou cover him; and that thou hide not thyself from thine own flesh?
    Then shall thy light break forth as the morning, and thine health shall spring forth speedily: and thy righteousness shall go before thee; the glory of the LORD shall be thy rereward.   ISAIAH 58:7–8

Every man according as he purposeth in his heart, so let him give; not grudgingly, or of necessity: for God loveth a cheerful giver.   2 CORINTHIANS 9:7

Blessed is he that considereth the poor: the LORD will deliver him in time of trouble.

The LORD will preserve him, and keep him alive; and he shall be blessed upon the earth: and thou wilt not deliver him unto the will of his enemies.

PSALM 41:1–2

HE THAT DESPISETH HIS NEIGHBOUR SINNETH: BUT HE THAT HATH MERCY ON THE POOR, HAPPY IS HE.
Proverbs 14:21

And he saw also a certain poor widow casting in thither two mites.

And he said, Of a truth I say unto you, that this poor widow hath cast in more than they all:

For all these have of their abundance cast in unto the offerings of God: but she of her penury hath cast in all the living that she had.

LUKE 21:2–4

For whosoever shall give you a cup of water to drink in my name, because ye belong to Christ, verily I say unto you, he shall not lose his reward. MARK 9:41

Then shall the King say unto them on his right hand, Come, ye blessed of my Father, inherit the kingdom prepared for you from the foundation of the world:

For I was an hungred, and ye gave me meat: I was thirsty, and ye gave me drink: I was a stranger, and ye took me in:

Naked, and ye clothed me: I was sick, and ye visited me: I was in prison, and ye came unto me.

Then shall the righteous answer him, saying, Lord, when saw we thee an hungred, and fed thee? or thirsty, and gave thee drink?

When saw we thee a stranger, and took thee in? or naked, and clothed thee?

Or when saw we thee sick, or in prison, and came unto thee?

And the King shall answer and say unto them, Verily I say unto you, Inasmuch as ye have done it unto one of the least of these my brethren, ye have done it unto me.   MATTHEW 25:34–40

Every man shall give as he is able, according to the blessing of the LORD thy God which he hath given thee.   DEUTERONOMY 16:17

Give, and it shall be given unto you; good measure, pressed down, and shaken together, and running over, shall men give into your bosom. For with the same measure that ye mete withal it shall be measured to you again.   LUKE 6:38

For ye know the grace of our Lord Jesus Christ, that, though he was rich, yet for your sakes he became poor, that ye through his poverty might be rich.

2 CORINTHIANS 8:9

HE THAT HATH PITY
UPON THE POOR
LENDETH UNTO THE LORD;
AND THAT WHICH HE
HATH GIVEN WILL HE
PAY HIM AGAIN.
Proverbs 19:17

He hath dispersed, he hath given to the poor; his righteousness endureth for ever; his horn shall be exalted with honour. PSALM 112:9

Charge them that are rich in this world, that they be not highminded, nor trust in uncertain riches, but in the living God, who giveth us richly all things to enjoy;

That they do good, that they be rich in good works, ready to distribute, willing to communicate. . .

1 TIMOTHY 6:17–18

I have shewed you all things, how that so labouring ye ought to support the weak, and to remember the words of the Lord Jesus, how he said, It is more blessed to give than to receive. ACTS 20:35

But when thou makest a feast, call the poor, the maimed, the lame, the blind:

And thou shalt be blessed; for they cannot recompense thee: for thou shalt be recompensed at the resurrection of the just. LUKE 14:13–14

Withhold not good from them to whom it is due, when it is in the power of thine hand to do it.

Say not unto thy neighbour, Go, and come again, and to morrow I will give; when thou hast it by thee. PROVERBS 3:27–28

He answereth and saith unto them, He that hath two coats, let him impart to him that hath none; and he that hath meat, let him do likewise.

LUKE 3:11

GOD LOVES US
THE WAY WE ARE
BUT HE LOVES US TOO MUCH
TO LEAVE US THAT WAY.
Leighton Ford

Herein is love, not that we loved God, but that he loved us, and sent his Son to be the propitiation for our sins.   1 JOHN 4:10

For God so loved the world, that he gave his only begotten Son, that whosoever believeth in him should not perish, but have everlasting life.
JOHN 3:16

The LORD preserveth all them that love him.
PSALM 145:20

But God commendeth his love toward us, in that, while we were yet sinners, Christ died for us.

ROMANS 5:8

In this was manifested the love of God toward us, because that God sent his only begotten Son into the world, that we might live through him.

1 JOHN 4:9

I will heal their backsliding, I will love them freely: for mine anger is turned away from him.

HOSEA 14:4

For I am persuaded, that neither death, nor life, nor angels, nor principalities, nor powers, nor things present, nor things to come,

Nor height, nor depth, nor any other creature, shall be able to separate us from the love of God, which is in Christ Jesus our Lord.

ROMANS 8:38–39

BEHOLD,
WHAT MANNER OF LOVE
THE FATHER HATH
BESTOWED UPON US,
THAT WE SHOULD BE
CALLED THE SONS OF GOD.
1 John 3:1

For the Father himself loveth you, because ye have loved me, and have believed that I came out from God.

JOHN 16:27

GOD'S PROVISION

HE WHO DOES GOOD
FOR GOD'S SAKE SEEKS
NEITHER PRAISE NOR REWARD,
BUT HE IS SURE OF
BOTH IN THE END.
William Penn

The young lions do lack, and suffer hunger: but they that seek the LORD shall not want any good thing.
PSALM 34:10

Charge them that are rich in this world, that they be not highminded, nor trust in uncertain riches, but in the living God, who giveth us richly all things to enjoy.
1 TIMOTHY 6:17

Therefore I say unto you, Take no thought for your life, what ye shall eat, or what ye shall drink; nor yet for your body, what ye shall put on. Is not the life more than meat, and the body than raiment?

Behold the fowls of the air: for they sow not, neither do they reap, nor gather into barns; yet your heavenly Father feedeth them. Are ye not much better than they?

Which of you by taking thought can add one cubit unto his stature?

And why take ye thought for raiment? Consider the lilies of the field, how they grow; they toil not, neither do they spin:

And yet I say unto you, That even Solomon in all his glory was not arrayed like one of these.

Wherefore, if God so clothe the grass of the field, which to day is, and to morrow is cast into the oven, shall he not much more clothe you, O ye of little faith?

Therefore take no thought, saying, What shall we eat? or, What shall we drink? or, Wherewithal shall we be clothed?

(For after all these things do the Gentiles seek:) for your heavenly Father knoweth that ye have need of all these things.

But seek ye first the kingdom of God, and his righteousness; and all these things shall be added unto you.   MATTHEW 6:25–33

He hath given meat unto them that fear him.
                                            PSALM 111:5

WE HAVE BEEN A
MOST FAVORED PEOPLE.
WE OUGHT TO BE A
MOST GRATEFUL PEOPLE.
Calvin Coolidge

And he took the cup, and gave thanks, and gave it to them, saying, Drink ye all of it.   MATTHEW 26:27

I will praise thee, O LORD, with my whole heart; I will shew forth all thy marvellous works.

I will be glad and rejoice in thee: I will sing praise to thy name, O thou most High.   PSALM 9:1–2

In every thing give thanks: for this is the will of God in Christ Jesus concerning you.
1 THESSALONIANS 5:18

Blessed be the LORD, that hath given rest unto his people Israel, according to all that he promised: there hath not failed one word of all his good promise, which he promised by the hand of Moses his servant. 1 KINGS 8:56

That I may publish with the voice of thanksgiving, and tell of all thy wondrous works. PSALM 26:7

O LORD, thou hast brought up my soul from the grave: thou hast kept me alive, that I should not go down to the pit. PSALM 30:3

He that regardeth the day, regardeth it unto the Lord; and he that regardeth not the day, to the Lord he doth not regard it. He that eateth, eateth to the Lord, for he giveth God thanks; and he that eateth not, to the Lord he eateth not, and giveth God thanks. ROMANS 14:6

Thou hast turned for me my mourning into dancing: thou hast put off my sackcloth, and girded me with gladness;

To the end that my glory may sing praise to thee, and not be silent. O LORD my God, I will give thanks unto thee for ever. PSALM 30:11–12

And he took the seven loaves and the fishes, and gave thanks, and brake them, and gave to his disciples, and the disciples to the multitude. MATTHEW 15:36

And they, continuing daily with one accord in the temple, and breaking bread from house to house, did eat their meat with gladness and singleness of heart,

Praising God, and having favour with all the people. And the Lord added to the church daily such as should be saved.   ACTS 2:46–47

I will mention the lovingkindnesses of the LORD, and the praises of the LORD, according to all that the LORD hath bestowed on us, and the great goodness toward the house of Israel, which he hath bestowed on them according to his mercies, and according to the multitude of his lovingkindnesses.
                                                    ISAIAH 63:7

BLESSED BE THE LORD,
WHO DAILY LOADETH US
WITH BENEFITS,
EVEN THE GOD
OF OUR SALVATION.
SELAH.
Psalm 68:19

Many, O LORD my God, are thy wonderful works which thou hast done, and thy thoughts which are to us-ward: they cannot be reckoned up in order unto thee: if I would declare and speak of them, they are more than can be numbered. PSALM 40:5

O give thanks unto the LORD; for he is good: for his mercy endureth for ever.   PSALM 136:1

Giving thanks always for all things unto God and the Father in the name of our Lord Jesus Christ.

EPHESIANS 5:20

I thank thee, and praise thee, O thou God of my fathers, who hast given me wisdom and might, and hast made known unto me now what we desired of thee: for thou hast now made known unto us the king's matter.

DANIEL 2:23

It is a good thing to give thanks unto the LORD, and to sing praises unto thy name, O most High:

To shew forth thy lovingkindness in the morning, and thy faithfulness every night.

PSALM 92:1–2

AND HE THAT
DOES ONE FAULT AT FIRST
AND LIES TO HIDE IT,
MAKES IT TWO.

Isaac Watts

Ye shall do no unrighteousness in judgment, in meteyard, in weight, or in measure.

Just balances, just weights, a just ephah, and a just hin, shall ye have: I am the LORD your God, which brought you out of the land of Egypt.

LEVITICUS 19:35–36

Thou knowest the commandments, Do not commit adultery, Do not kill, Do not steal, Do not bear false witness, Defraud not, Honour thy father and mother.

MARK 10:19

Pray for us: for we trust we have a good conscience, in all things willing to live honestly.

HEBREWS 13:18

Thou shalt not have in thy bag divers weights, a great and a small.

Thou shalt not have in thine house divers measures, a great and a small.

But thou shalt have a perfect and just weight, a perfect and just measure shalt thou have: that thy days may be lengthened in the land which the LORD thy God giveth thee.

For all that do such things, and all that do unrighteously, are an abomination unto the LORD thy God. DEUTERONOMY 25:13–16

PROVIDING FOR HONEST
THINGS, NOT ONLY IN THE
SIGHT OF THE LORD, BUT
ALSO IN THE SIGHT OF MEN.
2 Corinthians 8:21

And as ye would that men should do to you, do ye also to them likewise. LUKE 6:31

He that putteth not out his money to usury, nor taketh reward against the innocent. He that doeth these things shall never be moved. PSALM 15:5

Ye shall not steal, neither deal falsely, neither lie one to another. LEVITICUS 19:11

And herein do I exercise myself, to have always a conscience void of offence toward God, and toward men. ACTS 24:16

He that walketh righteously, and speaketh uprightly; he that despiseth the gain of oppressions, that shaketh his hands from holding of bribes, that stoppeth his ears from hearing of blood, and shutteth his eyes from seeing evil;

He shall dwell on high: his place of defence shall be the munitions of rocks: bread shall be given him; his waters shall be sure. ISAIAH 33:15–16

Therefore all things whatsoever ye would that men should do to you, do ye even so to them: for this is the law and the prophets. MATTHEW 7:12

Then came also publicans to be baptized, and said unto him, Master, what shall we do?

And he said unto them, Exact no more than that which is appointed you. LUKE 3:12–13

Lie not one to another, seeing that ye have put off the old man with his deeds;

And have put on the new man, which is renewed in knowledge after the image of him that created him. COLOSSIANS 3:9–10

He that hath clean hands, and a pure heart; who hath not lifted up his soul unto vanity, nor sworn deceitfully. PSALM 24:4

Receive us; we have wronged no man, we have corrupted no man, we have defrauded no man.

2 CORINTHIANS 7:2

A FALSE BALANCE IS ABOMINATION TO THE LORD: BUT A JUST WEIGHT IS HIS DELIGHT.
Proverbs 11:1

My righteousness I hold fast, and will not let it go: my heart shall not reproach me so long as I live.

JOB 27:6

Servants, obey in all things your masters according to the flesh; not with eyeservice, as menpleasers; but in singleness of heart, fearing God.

COLOSSIANS 3:22

EVERYTHING THAT IS
DONE IN THE WORLD
IS DONE BY HOPE.
Martin Luther

In hope of eternal life, which God, that cannot lie, promised before the world began.   TITUS 1:2

But Christ as a son over his own house; whose house are we, if we hold fast the confidence and the rejoicing of the hope firm unto the end.

HEBREWS 3:6

And hope maketh not ashamed; because the love of God is shed abroad in our hearts by the Holy Ghost which is given unto us.   ROMANS 5:5

That by two immutable things, in which it was impossible for God to lie, we might have a strong consolation, who have fled for refuge to lay hold upon the hope set before us:

Which hope we have as an anchor of the soul, both sure and stedfast, and which entereth into that within the veil. HEBREWS 6:18–19

Blessed is the man that trusteth in the LORD, and whose hope the LORD is. JEREMIAH 17:7

Now the God of hope fill you with all joy and peace in believing, that ye may abound in hope, through the power of the Holy Ghost. ROMANS 15:13

To whom God would make known what is the riches of the glory of this mystery among the Gentiles; which is Christ in you, the hope of glory. COLOSSIANS 1:27

Who by him do believe in God, that raised him up from the dead, and gave him glory; that your faith and hope might be in God. 1 PETER 1:21

It is good that a man should both hope and quietly wait for the salvation of the LORD. LAMENTATIONS 3:26

And have hope toward God, which they themselves also allow, that there shall be a resurrection of the dead, both of the just and unjust. ACTS 24:15

And we desire that every one of you do shew the same diligence to the full assurance of hope unto the end.   HEBREWS 6:11

Who against hope believed in hope, that he might become the father of many nations, according to that which was spoken, So shall thy seed be.
                                        ROMANS 4:18

BUT I WILL HOPE CONTINUALLY,
AND WILL YET PRAISE THEE
MORE AND MORE.
Psalm 71:14

There is one body, and one Spirit, even as ye are called in one hope of your calling.   EPHESIANS 4:4

For we are saved by hope: but hope that is seen is not hope: for what a man seeth, why doth he yet hope for?
    But if we hope for that we see not, then do we with patience wait for it.   ROMANS 8:24–25

LORD, I have hoped for thy salvation, and done thy commandments.   PSALM 119:166

According to my earnest expectation and my hope, that in nothing I shall be ashamed, but that with all boldness, as always, so now also Christ shall be magnified in my body, whether it be by life, or by death.   PHILIPPIANS 1:20

Why art thou cast down, O my soul? and why art thou disquieted within me? hope thou in God: for I shall yet praise him, who is the health of my countenance, and my God. PSALM 42:11

Seeing then that we have such hope, we use great plainness of speech. 2 CORINTHIANS 3:12

The eyes of your understanding being enlightened; that ye may know what is the hope of his calling, and what the riches of the glory of his inheritance in the saints. EPHESIANS 1:18

For the hope which is laid up for you in heaven, whereof ye heard before in the word of the truth of the gospel. COLOSSIANS 1:5

Now faith is the substance of things hoped for, the evidence of things not seen. HEBREWS 11:1

For the needy shall not alway be forgotten: the expectation of the poor shall not perish for ever.
PSALM 9:18

FOR WE THROUGH
THE SPIRIT WAIT
FOR THE HOPE OF
RIGHTEOUSNESS BY FAITH.
Galatians 5:5

And every man that hath this hope in him purifieth himself, even as he is pure. 1 JOHN 3:3

NO MAN IS GREAT IF
HE THINKS HE IS.
Will Rogers

Whosoever therefore shall humble himself as this little child, the same is greatest in the kingdom of heaven. MATTHEW 18:4

When men are cast down, then thou shalt say, There is lifting up; and he shall save the humble person.
JOB 22:29

LORD, my heart is not haughty, nor mine eyes lofty: neither do I exercise myself in great matters, or in things too high for me. PSALM 131:1

By humility and the fear of the LORD are riches, and honour, and life. PROVERBS 22:4

But he giveth more grace. Wherefore he saith, God resisteth the proud, but giveth grace unto the humble. JAMES 4:6

Blessed are the poor in spirit: for theirs is the kingdom of heaven. MATTHEW 5:3

Hearken to me, ye that follow after righteousness, ye that seek the LORD: look unto the rock whence ye are hewn, and to the hole of the pit whence ye are digged. ISAIAH 51:1

LORD, thou hast heard the desire of the humble: thou wilt prepare their heart, thou wilt cause thine ear to hear. PSALM 10:17

The fear of the LORD is the instruction of wisdom; and before honour is humility. PROVERBS 15:33

Yea, all of you be subject one to another, and be clothed with humility: for God resisteth the proud, and giveth grace to the humble.
Humble yourselves therefore under the mighty hand of God, that he may exalt you in due time. 1 PETER 5:5–6

And whosoever shall exalt himself shall be abased; and he that shall humble himself shall be exalted. MATTHEW 23:12

Humble yourselves in the sight of the Lord, and he shall lift you up. JAMES 4:10

But made himself of no reputation, and took upon him the form of a servant, and was made in the likeness of men:

And being found in fashion as a man, he humbled himself, and became obedient unto death, even the death of the cross.

Wherefore God also hath highly exalted him, and given him a name which is above every name.
PHILIPPIANS 2:7–9

SURELY HE SCORNETH
THE SCORNERS:
BUT HE GIVETH GRACE
UNTO THE LOWLY.
Proverbs 3:34

Though the LORD be high, yet hath he respect unto the lowly: but the proud he knoweth afar off.
PSALM 138:6

When he maketh inquisition for blood, he remembereth them: he forgetteth not the cry of the humble.
PSALM 9:12

Behold even to the moon, and it shineth not; yea, the stars are not pure in his sight.

How much less man, that is a worm? and the son of man, which is a worm? JOB 25:5–6

Better it is to be of an humble spirit with the lowly, than to divide the spoil with the proud.

PROVERBS 16:19

For thus saith the high and lofty One that inhabiteth eternity, whose name is Holy; I dwell in the high and holy place, with him also that is of a contrite and humble spirit, to revive the spirit of the humble, and to revive the heart of the contrite ones. ISAIAH 57:15

When pride cometh, then cometh shame: but with the lowly is wisdom. PROVERBS 11:2

Let another man praise thee, and not thine own mouth; a stranger, and not thine own lips.

PROVERBS 27:2

Let no man deceive himself. If any man among you seemeth to be wise in this world, let him become a fool, that he may be wise. 1 CORINTHIANS 3:18

Be not rash with thy mouth, and let not thine heart be hasty to utter any thing before God: for God is in heaven, and thou upon earth: therefore let thy words be few. ECCLESIASTES 5:2

A man's pride shall bring him low: but honour shall uphold the humble in spirit. PROVERBS 29:23

Boast not thyself of tomorrow; for thou knowest not what a day may bring forth. PROVERBS 27:1

Be not wise in your own conceits.   ROMANS 12:16

If I must needs glory, I will glory of the things which concern mine infirmities.   2 CORINTHIANS 11:30

Shall the ax boast itself against him that heweth therewith? or shall the saw magnify itself against him that shaketh it? as if the rod should shake itself against them that lift it up, or as if the staff should lift up itself, as if it were no wood.   ISAIAH 10:15

And base things of the world, and things which are despised, hath God chosen, yea, and things which are not, to bring to nought things that are:
   That no flesh should glory in his presence.
                                        1 CORINTHIANS 1:28–29

EVEN SO THE TONGUE
IS A LITTLE MEMBER,
AND BOASTETH
GREAT THINGS.
BEHOLD,
HOW GREAT A MATTER A
LITTLE FIRE KINDLETH!
James 3:5

Thus saith the LORD, Let not the wise man glory in his wisdom, neither let the mighty man glory in his might, let not the rich man glory in his riches.
                                        JEREMIAH 9:23

Do not let
your happiness depend on
something you may lose. . .
only [upon] the Beloved
who will never pass away.

C. S. Lewis

And the angel said unto them, Fear not: for, behold, I bring you good tidings of great joy, which shall be to all people. LUKE 2:10

The LORD is my strength and my shield; my heart trusted in him, and I am helped: therefore my heart greatly rejoiceth; and with my song will I praise him. PSALM 28:7

Is any merry? let him sing psalms. JAMES 5:13

Rejoice in the Lord alway: and again I say, Rejoice.
PHILIPPIANS 4:4

Hitherto have ye asked nothing in my name: ask, and ye shall receive, that your joy may be full.
JOHN 16:24

Be glad in the LORD, and rejoice, ye righteous: and shout for joy, all ye that are upright in heart.
PSALM 32:11

In the transgression of an evil man there is a snare: but the righteous doth sing and rejoice.
PROVERBS 29:6

As sorrowful, yet alway rejoicing; as poor, yet making many rich; as having nothing, and yet possessing all things.   2 CORINTHIANS 6:10

My lips shall greatly rejoice when I sing unto thee; and my soul, which thou hast redeemed.
PSALM 71:23

Therefore the redeemed of the LORD shall return, and come with singing unto Zion; and everlasting joy shall be upon their head: they shall obtain gladness and joy; and sorrow and mourning shall flee away.   ISAIAH 51:11

A merry heart doeth good like a medicine: but a broken spirit drieth the bones.   PROVERBS 17:22

His lord said unto him, Well done, thou good and faithful servant: thou hast been faithful over a few things, I will make thee ruler over many things: enter thou into the joy of thy lord.   MATTHEW 25:21

Rejoice ye in that day, and leap for joy: for, behold, your reward is great in heaven: for in the like manner did their fathers unto the prophets.

LUKE 6:23

MAKE A JOYFUL NOISE
UNTO THE LORD,
ALL YE LANDS.
SERVE THE LORD
WITH GLADNESS:
COME BEFORE HIS PRESENCE
WITH SINGING.
Psalm 100:1–2

And now come I to thee; and these things I speak in the world, that they might have my joy fulfilled in themselves.   JOHN 17:13

All the days of the afflicted are evil: but he that is of a merry heart hath a continual feast.

PROVERBS 15:15

Let all those that seek thee rejoice and be glad in thee: let such as love thy salvation say continually, The LORD be magnified.   PSALM 40:16

And not only so, but we also joy in God through our Lord Jesus Christ, by whom we have now received the atonement.   ROMANS 5:11

Not for that we have dominion over your faith, but are helpers of your joy: for by faith ye stand.
                                          2 CORINTHIANS 1:24

FOR OUR HEART SHALL
REJOICE IN HIM,
BECAUSE WE HAVE
TRUSTED IN HIS
HOLY NAME.
Psalm 33:21

Speaking to yourselves in psalms and hymns and spiritual songs, singing and making melody in your heart to the Lord.   EPHESIANS 5:19

I will greatly rejoice in the LORD, my soul shall be joyful in my God; for he hath clothed me with the garments of salvation, he hath covered me with the robe of righteousness, as a bridegroom decketh himself with ornaments, and as a bride adorneth herself with her jewels.   ISAIAH 61:10

JUSTICE

WE ARE ALWAYS
LOOKING FOR JUSTICE,
YET THE ESSENCE OF
THE TEACHING OF
THE SERMON ON THE MOUNT IS—
NEVER LOOK FOR JUSTICE,
BUT NEVER CEASE TO GIVE IT.

Oswald Chambers

Thou shalt not raise a false report: put not thine hand with the wicked to be an unrighteous witness.

Thou shalt not follow a multitude to do evil; neither shalt thou speak in a cause to decline after many to wrest judgment:

Neither shalt thou countenance a poor man in his cause.   EXODUS 23:1–3

Thou shalt not defraud thy neighbour, neither rob him: the wages of him that is hired shall not abide with thee all night until the morning.

Thou shalt not curse the deaf, nor put a stumblingblock before the blind, but shalt fear thy God: I am the LORD.

Ye shall do no unrighteousness in judgment: thou shalt not respect the person of the poor, nor honour the person of the mighty: but in righteousness shalt thou judge thy neighbour.

LEVITICUS 19:13–15

DOTH OUR LAW JUDGE ANY MAN, BEFORE IT HEAR HIM, AND KNOW WHAT HE DOETH?

John 7:51

If there be a controversy between men, and they come unto judgment, that the judges may judge them; then they shall justify the righteous, and condemn the wicked.   DEUTERONOMY 25:1

How long will ye judge unjustly, and accept the persons of the wicked? Selah.

Defend the poor and fatherless: do justice to the afflicted and needy.

Deliver the poor and needy: rid them out of the hand of the wicked.   PSALM 82:2–4

But if ye had known what this meaneth, I will have mercy, and not sacrifice, ye would not have condemned the guiltless. MATTHEW 12:7

And moreover I saw under the sun the place of judgment, that wickedness was there; and the place of righteousness, that iniquity was there.

I said in mine heart, God shall judge the righteous and the wicked: for there is a time there for every purpose and for every work.

ECCLESIASTES 3:16–17

Thus saith the LORD, Keep ye judgment, and do justice: for my salvation is near to come, and my righteousness to be revealed. ISAIAH 56:1

Thus saith the LORD; Execute ye judgment and righteousness, and deliver the spoiled out of the hand of the oppressor: and do no wrong, do no violence to the stranger, the fatherless, nor the widow, neither shed innocent blood in this place. JEREMIAH 22:3

That no man go beyond and defraud his brother in any matter: because that the Lord is the avenger of all such, as we also have forewarned you and testified.

For God hath not called us unto uncleanness, but unto holiness.

He therefore that despiseth, despiseth not man, but God, who hath also given unto us his holy Spirit.

1 THESSALONIANS 4:6–8

To turn aside the right of a man before the face of the most High,

To subvert a man in his cause, the Lord approveth not. LAMENTATIONS 3:35–36

Judge not according to the appearance, but judge righteous judgment. JOHN 7:24

He that justifieth the wicked, and he that condemneth the just, even they both are abomination to the LORD. PROVERBS 17:15

Thou shalt not wrest the judgment of thy poor in his cause.

Keep thee far from a false matter; and the innocent and righteous slay thou not: for I will not justify the wicked.

And thou shalt take no gift: for the gift blindeth the wise, and perverteth the words of the righteous. EXODUS 23:6–8

Learn to do well; seek judgment, relieve the oppressed, judge the fatherless, plead for the widow. ISAIAH 1:17

BIG JOBS USUALLY GO TO THE MEN WHO PROVE THEIR ABILITY TO OUTGROW SMALL ONES.

Ralph Waldo Emerson

But if any provide not for his own, and specially for those of his own house, he hath denied the faith, and is worse than an infidel.   1 TIMOTHY 5:8

He becometh poor that dealeth with a slack hand: but the hand of the diligent maketh rich.

PROVERBS 10:4

The soul of the sluggard desireth, and hath nothing: but the soul of the diligent shall be made fat.

PROVERBS 13:4

Not slothful in business; fervent in spirit; serving the Lord.   ROMANS 12:11

Whatsoever thy hand findeth to do, do it with thy might; for there is no work, nor device, nor knowledge, nor wisdom, in the grave, whither thou goest.
ECCLESIASTES 9:10

Let him that stole steal no more: but rather let him labour, working with his hands the thing which is good, that he may have to give to him that needeth.
EPHESIANS 4:28

He that tilleth his land shall be satisfied with bread: but he that followeth vain persons is void of understanding.   PROVERBS 12:11

For even when we were with you, this we commanded you, that if any would not work, neither should he eat.   2 THESSALONIANS 3:10

Love not sleep, lest thou come to poverty; open thine eyes, and thou shalt be satisfied with bread.
PROVERBS 20:13

And that ye study to be quiet, and to do your own business, and to work with your own hands, as we commanded you;
That ye may walk honestly toward them that are without, and that ye may have lack of nothing.
1 THESSALONIANS 4:11–12

The spider taketh hold with her hands, and is in kings' palaces.   PROVERBS 30:28

I know that there is no good in them, but for a man to rejoice, and to do good in his life.

And also that every man should eat and drink, and enjoy the good of all his labour, it is the gift of God.   ECCLESIASTES 3:12–13

THE HAND OF THE DILIGENT SHALL BEAR RULE: BUT THE SLOTHFUL SHALL BE UNDER TRIBUTE.
Proverbs 12:24

Wealth gotten by vanity shall be diminished: but he that gathereth by labour shall increase.
                          PROVERBS 13:11

For thou shalt eat the labour of thine hands: happy shalt thou be, and it shall be well with thee.
                          PSALM 128:2

LEADERSHIP IS
GETTING SOMEONE TO DO
WHAT THEY DON'T WANT TO DO,
TO ACHIEVE WHAT
THEY WANT TO ACHIEVE.

Tom Landry

Feed the flock of God which is among you, taking the oversight thereof, not by constraint, but willingly; not for filthy lucre, but of a ready mind;

Neither as being lords over God's heritage, but being ensamples to the flock.

And when the chief Shepherd shall appear, ye shall receive a crown of glory that fadeth not away.

1 PETER 5:2–4

But thou, O man of God, flee these things; and follow after righteousness, godliness, faith, love, patience, meekness.

Fight the good fight of faith, lay hold on eternal life, whereunto thou art also called, and hast professed a good profession before many witnesses.

I give thee charge in the sight of God, who quickeneth all things, and before Christ Jesus, who before Pontius Pilate witnessed a good confession;

That thou keep this commandment without spot, unrebukeable, until the appearing of our Lord Jesus Christ.   1 TIMOTHY 6:11–14

Take heed therefore unto yourselves, and to all the flock, over the which the Holy Ghost hath made you overseers, to feed the church of God, which he hath purchased with his own blood.   ACTS 20:28

NEGLECT NOT THE GIFT THAT IS IN THEE, WHICH WAS GIVEN THEE BY PROPHECY.
1 Timothy 4:14

And they that have believing masters, let them not despise them, because they are brethren; but rather do them service, because they are faithful and beloved, partakers of the benefit. These things teach and exhort.   1 TIMOTHY 6:2

Let the deacons be the husbands of one wife, ruling their children and their own houses well.

For they that have used the office of a deacon well purchase to themselves a good degree, and great boldness in the faith which is in Christ Jesus.
1 TIMOTHY 3:12–13

A bishop then must be blameless, the husband of one wife, vigilant, sober, of good behaviour, given to hospitality, apt to teach;

Not given to wine, no striker, not greedy of filthy lucre; but patient, not a brawler, not covetous;

One that ruleth well his own house, having his children in subjection with all gravity;

(For if a man know not how to rule his own house, how shall he take care of the church of God?)

Not a novice, lest being lifted up with pride he fall into the condemnation of the devil.

Moreover he must have a good report of them which are without; lest he fall into reproach and the snare of the devil.
1 TIMOTHY 3:2–7

Whosoever transgresseth, and abideth not in the doctrine of Christ, hath not God. He that abideth in the doctrine of Christ, he hath both the Father and the Son.

If there come any unto you, and bring not this doctrine, receive him not into your house, neither bid him God speed:

For he that biddeth him God speed is partaker of his evil deeds.
2 JOHN 9–11

Let no man despise thy youth; but be thou an example of the believers, in word, in conversation, in charity, in spirit, in faith, in purity.

1 TIMOTHY 4:12

HOLDING FAST
THE FAITHFUL WORD AS
HE HATH BEEN TAUGHT,
THAT HE MAY BE ABLE BY
SOUND DOCTRINE BOTH
TO EXHORT AND TO
CONVINCE THE GAINSAYERS.
Titus 1:9

Now then we are ambassadors for Christ, as though God did beseech you by us: we pray you in Christ's stead, be ye reconciled to God.

2 CORINTHIANS 5:20

THE KINGDOM OF HEAVEN
IS NOT COME EVEN WHEN
GOD'S WILL IS OUR LAW;
IT IS FULLY COME WHEN
GOD'S WILL IS OUR WILL.

George MacDonald

And Jesus answered him, The first of all the commandments is, Hear, O Israel; The Lord our God is one Lord:

And thou shalt love the Lord thy God with all thy heart, and with all thy soul, and with all thy mind, and with all thy strength: this is the first commandment.

And the second is like, namely this, Thou shalt love thy neighbour as thyself. There is none other commandment greater than these.   MARK 12:29–31

Jesus said unto them, If God were your Father, ye would love me: for I proceeded forth and came from God; neither came I of myself, but he sent me.

JOHN 8:42

The LORD hath appeared of old unto me, saying, Yea, I have loved thee with an everlasting love: therefore with lovingkindness have I drawn thee.

JEREMIAH 31:3

That Christ may dwell in your hearts by faith; that ye, being rooted and grounded in love,

May be able to comprehend with all saints what is the breadth, and length, and depth, and height;

And to know the love of Christ, which passeth knowledge, that ye might be filled with all the fulness of God.

EPHESIANS 3:17–19

Take good heed therefore unto yourselves, that ye love the LORD your God.

JOSHUA 23:11

As the Father hath loved me, so have I loved you: continue ye in my love.

JOHN 15:9

For God is not unrighteous to forget your work and labour of love, which ye have shewed toward his name.

HEBREWS 6:10

And thou shalt love the LORD thy God with all thine heart, and with all thy soul, and with all thy might.

DEUTERONOMY 6:5

Love not the world, neither the things that are in the world. If any man love the world, the love of the Father is not in him. 1 JOHN 2:15

Delight thyself also in the LORD; and he shall give thee the desires of thine heart. PSALM 37:4

And we know that all things work together for good to them that love God, to them who are the called according to his purpose. ROMANS 8:28

MY SON,
GIVE ME THINE HEART,
AND LET THINE EYES
OBSERVE MY WAYS.
Proverbs 23:26

And I have declared unto them thy name, and will declare it: that the love wherewith thou hast loved me may be in them, and I in them. JOHN 17:26

I will declare thy name unto my brethren: in the midst of the congregation will I praise thee.
PSALM 22:22

Keep yourselves in the love of God, looking for the mercy of our Lord Jesus Christ unto eternal life.
JUDE 21

The LORD preserveth all them that love him.
PSALM 145:20

And we have known and believed the love that God hath to us. God is love; and he that dwelleth in love dwelleth in God, and God in him.

Herein is our love made perfect, that we may have boldness in the day of judgment: because as he is, so are we in this world.

There is no fear in love; but perfect love casteth out fear: because fear hath torment. He that feareth is not made perfect in love.

We love him, because he first loved us.

1 JOHN 4:16–19

He that hath my commandments, and keepeth them, he it is that loveth me: and he that loveth me shall be loved of my Father, and I will love him, and will manifest myself to him.   JOHN 14:21

I love them that love me; and those that seek me early shall find me.   PROVERBS 8:17

But if any man love God, the same is known of him.

1 CORINTHIANS 8:3

LOVE MORE PERSONS MORE—
LOVE THEM MORE IMPERSONALLY,
MORE UNSELFISHLY,
WITHOUT THOUGHT OF RETURN.
THE RETURN, NEVER FEAR,
WILL TAKE CARE OF ITSELF.

Henry Drummond

And now abideth faith, hope, charity, these three; but the greatest of these is charity.

1 CORINTHIANS 13:13

Thou shalt not avenge, nor bear any grudge against the children of thy people, but thou shalt love thy neighbour as thyself: I am the LORD.

LEVITICUS 19:18

Ye have heard that it hath been said, Thou shalt love thy neighbour, and hate thine enemy.

But I say unto you, Love your enemies, bless them that curse you, do good to them that hate you, and pray for them which despitefully use you, and persecute you;

That ye may be the children of your Father which is in heaven: for he maketh his sun to rise on the evil and on the good, and sendeth rain on the just and on the unjust.   MATTHEW 5:43–45

FOR THIS IS THE MESSAGE
THAT YE HEARD FROM
THE BEGINNING,
THAT WE SHOULD
LOVE ONE ANOTHER.
1 John 3:11

Though I speak with the tongues of men and of angels, and have not charity, I am become as sounding brass, or a tinkling cymbal.

And though I have the gift of prophecy, and understand all mysteries, and all knowledge; and though I have all faith, so that I could remove mountains, and have not charity, I am nothing.

And though I bestow all my goods to feed the poor, and though I give my body to be burned, and have not charity, it profiteth me nothing.

1 CORINTHIANS 13:1–3

He that loveth not knoweth not God; for God is love.   1 JOHN 4:8

If a man say, I love God, and hateth his brother, he is a liar: for he that loveth not his brother whom he hath seen, how can he love God whom he hath not seen?

And this commandment have we from him, That he who loveth God love his brother also.

1 JOHN 4:20–21

In this the children of God are manifest, and the children of the devil: whosoever doeth not righteousness is not of God, neither he that loveth not his brother.

1 JOHN 3:10

Leave there thy gift before the altar, and go thy way; first be reconciled to thy brother, and then come and offer thy gift.

MATTHEW 5:24

This is my commandment, That ye love one another, as I have loved you.

Greater love hath no man than this, that a man lay down his life for his friends.

JOHN 15:12–13

I speak to your shame. Is it so, that there is not a wise man among you? no, not one that shall be able to judge between his brethren?

But brother goeth to law with brother, and that before the unbelievers.

Now therefore there is utterly a fault among you, because ye go to law one with another. Why do ye not rather take wrong? why do ye not rather suffer yourselves to be defrauded?

Nay, ye do wrong, and defraud, and that your brethren.

1 CORINTHIANS 6:5–8

Owe no man any thing, but to love one another: for he that loveth another hath fulfilled the law.

ROMANS 13:8

Be kindly affectioned one to another with brotherly love; in honour preferring one another.

ROMANS 12:10

AND LET US CONSIDER
ONE ANOTHER TO
PROVOKE UNTO LOVE
AND TO GOOD WORKS.
Hebrews 10:24

But as touching brotherly love ye need not that I write unto you: for ye yourselves are taught of God to love one another.   1 THESSALONIANS 4:9

For all the law is fulfilled in one word, even in this; Thou shalt love thy neighbour as thyself.

GALATIANS 5:14

Beloved, if God so loved us, we ought also to love one another.

No man hath seen God at any time. If we love one another, God dwelleth in us, and his love is perfected in us.   1 JOHN 4:11–12

Honour all men. Love the brotherhood. Fear God. Honour the king.   1 PETER 2:17

Hereby perceive we the love of God, because he laid down his life for us: and we ought to lay down our lives for the brethren.

But whoso hath this world's good, and seeth his brother have need, and shutteth up his bowels of compassion from him, how dwelleth the love of God in him?

My little children, let us not love in word, neither in tongue; but in deed and in truth.

And hereby we know that we are of the truth, and shall assure our hearts before him.

1 JOHN 3:16–19

And this I pray, that your love may abound yet more and more in knowledge and in all judgment.

PHILIPPIANS 1:9

And through thy knowledge shall the weak brother perish, for whom Christ died?

But when ye sin so against the brethren, and wound their weak conscience, ye sin against Christ.

1 CORINTHIANS 8:11–12

TEACH ME TO
FEEL ANOTHER'S WOE,
TO HIDE THE FAULT I SEE;
THAT MERCY I TO OTHERS SHOW,
THAT MERCY SHOW TO ME.

Alexander Pope

Behold, we count them happy which endure. Ye
have heard of the patience of Job, and have seen the
end of the Lord; that the Lord is very pitiful, and of
tender mercy.   JAMES 5:11

Thou art a God ready to pardon, gracious and merciful, slow to anger, and of great kindness.

NEHEMIAH 9:17

For God hath concluded them all in unbelief, that
he might have mercy upon all.   ROMANS 11:32

For thou, Lord, art good, and ready to forgive; and plenteous in mercy unto all them that call upon thee.   PSALM 86:5

He hath shewed thee, O man, what is good; and what doth the LORD require of thee, but to do justly, and to love mercy, and to walk humbly with thy God?   MICAH 6:8

Blessed be the God and Father of our Lord Jesus Christ, which according to his abundant mercy hath begotten us again unto a lively hope by the resurrection of Jesus Christ from the dead.   1 PETER 1:3

The LORD is good to all: and his tender mercies are over all his works.   PSALM 145:9

Let not mercy and truth forsake thee: bind them about thy neck; write them upon the table of thine heart:

So shalt thou find favour and good understanding in the sight of God and man. PROVERBS 3:3–4

BE YE THEREFORE
MERCIFUL,
AS YOUR FATHER
ALSO IS MERCIFUL.
Luke 6:36

And his mercy is on them that fear him from generation to generation.   LUKE 1:50

But God, who is rich in mercy, for his great love wherewith he loved us,

Even when we were dead in sins, hath quickened us together with Christ, (by grace ye are saved).
EPHESIANS 2:4–5

BLESSED ARE THE MERCIFUL: FOR THEY SHALL OBTAIN MERCY.
Matthew 5:7

Let the wicked forsake his way, and the unrighteous man his thoughts: and let him return unto the LORD, and he will have mercy upon him; and to our God, for he will abundantly pardon.   ISAIAH 55:7

Therefore turn thou to thy God: keep mercy and judgment, and wait on thy God continually.
HOSEA 12:6

He that covereth his sins shall not prosper: but whoso confesseth and forsaketh them shall have mercy.
PROVERBS 28:13

Mercy and truth are met together; righteousness and peace have kissed each other.   PSALM 85:10

But thou, O Lord, art a God full of compassion, and gracious, longsuffering, and plenteous in mercy and truth.   PSALM 86:15

Not by works of righteousness which we have done, but according to his mercy he saved us, by the washing of regeneration, and renewing of the Holy Ghost;

Which he shed on us abundantly through Jesus Christ our Saviour;

That being justified by his grace, we should be made heirs according to the hope of eternal life.

TITUS 3:5–7

For I will be merciful to their unrighteousness, and their sins and their iniquities will I remember no more.

In that he saith, A new covenant, he hath made the first old. Now that which decayeth and waxeth old is ready to vanish away.   HEBREWS 8:12–13

OBEDIENCE

ONLY HE WHO BELIEVES
IS OBEDIENT.
ONLY HE WHO IS OBEDIENT,
BELIEVES.
Dietrich Bonhoeffer

My son, forget not my law; but let thine heart keep
my commandments:

For length of days, and long life, and peace,
shall they add to thee. PROVERBS 3:1–2

Those things, which ye have both learned, and received, and heard, and seen in me, do: and the God
of peace shall be with you. PHILIPPIANS 4:9

If ye know these things, happy are ye if ye do them.
JOHN 13:17

If they obey and serve him, they shall spend their days in prosperity, and their years in pleasures.

JOB 36:11

But whoso looketh into the perfect law of liberty, and continueth therein, he being not a forgetful hearer, but a doer of the work, this man shall be blessed in his deed.

JAMES 1:25

Not every one that saith unto me, Lord, Lord, shall enter into the kingdom of heaven; but he that doeth the will of my Father which is in heaven.

MATTHEW 7:21

I command thee this day to love the LORD thy God, to walk in his ways, and to keep his commandments and his statutes and his judgments, that thou mayest live and multiply: and the LORD thy God shall bless thee in the land whither thou goest to possess it.

DEUTERONOMY 30:16

Let us hear the conclusion of the whole matter: Fear God, and keep his commandments: for this is the whole duty of man.

ECCLESIASTES 12:13

If ye keep my commandments, ye shall abide in my love; even as I have kept my Father's commandments, and abide in his love.

JOHN 15:10

And the world passeth away, and the lust thereof: but he that doeth the will of God abideth for ever.

1 JOHN 2:17

And Samuel said, Hath the LORD as great delight in burnt offerings and sacrifices, as in obeying the voice of the LORD? Behold, to obey is better than sacrifice, and to hearken than the fat of rams.

1 SAMUEL 15:22

Whosoever therefore shall break one of these least commandments, and shall teach men so, he shall be called the least in the kingdom of heaven: but whosoever shall do and teach them, the same shall be called great in the kingdom of heaven.

MATTHEW 5:19

FOR NOT THE HEARERS
OF THE LAW ARE JUST
BEFORE GOD,
BUT THE DOERS OF THE
LAW SHALL BE JUSTIFIED.
Romans 2:13

Keep therefore the words of this covenant, and do them, that ye may prosper in all that ye do.

DEUTERONOMY 29:9

Furthermore we have had fathers of our flesh which corrected us, and we gave them reverence: shall we not much rather be in subjection unto the Father of spirits, and live? HEBREWS 12:9

But he said, Yea rather, blessed are they that hear the word of God, and keep it. LUKE 11:28

OUR PATIENCE WILL ACHIEVE MORE THAN OUR FORCE.

Edmund Burke

For ye have need of patience, that, after ye have done the will of God, ye might receive the promise.

HEBREWS 10:36

Rest in the LORD, and wait patiently for him: fret not thyself because of him who prospereth in his way, because of the man who bringeth wicked devices to pass.

Cease from anger, and forsake wrath: fret not thyself in any wise to do evil.

For evildoers shall be cut off: but those that wait upon the LORD, they shall inherit the earth.

PSALM 37:7–9

Knowing this, that the trying of your faith worketh patience.

But let patience have her perfect work, that ye may be perfect and entire, wanting nothing.

JAMES 1:3–4

But that on the good ground are they, which in an honest and good heart, having heard the word, keep it, and bring forth fruit with patience.   LUKE 8:15

And let us not be weary in well doing: for in due season we shall reap, if we faint not.   GALATIANS 6:9

And not only so, but we glory in tribulations also: knowing that tribulation worketh patience;

And patience, experience; and experience, hope.

ROMANS 5:3–4

Here is the patience of the saints: here are they that keep the commandments of God, and the faith of Jesus.   REVELATION 14:12

But in all things approving ourselves as the ministers of God, in much patience, in afflictions, in necessities, in distresses.   2 CORINTHIANS 6:4

For whatsoever things were written aforetime were written for our learning, that we through patience and comfort of the scriptures might have hope.

Now the God of patience and consolation grant you to be likeminded one toward another according to Christ Jesus.   ROMANS 15:4–5

Now we exhort you, brethren, warn them that are unruly, comfort the feebleminded, support the weak, be patient toward all men.

1 THESSALONIANS 5:14

THAT YE BE NOT SLOTHFUL,
BUT FOLLOWERS OF THEM
WHO THROUGH FAITH
AND PATIENCE INHERIT
THE PROMISES.
Hebrews 6:12

And the Lord direct your hearts into the love of God, and into the patient waiting for Christ.

2 THESSALONIANS 3:5

Be patient therefore, brethren, unto the coming of the Lord. Behold, the husbandman waiteth for the precious fruit of the earth, and hath long patience for it, until he receive the early and latter rain.

Be ye also patient; stablish your hearts: for the coming of the Lord draweth nigh. JAMES 5:7–8

Wherefore seeing we also are compassed about with so great a cloud of witnesses, let us lay aside every weight, and the sin which doth so easily beset us, and let us run with patience the race that is set before us.

HEBREWS 12:1

To them who by patient continuance in well doing seek for glory and honour and immortality, eternal life. ROMANS 2:7

In your patience possess ye your souls.   LUKE 21:19

For what glory is it, if, when ye be buffeted for your faults, ye shall take it patiently? but if, when ye do well, and suffer for it, ye take it patiently, this is acceptable with God.   1 PETER 2:20

Better is the end of a thing than the beginning thereof: and the patient in spirit is better than the proud in spirit.

Be not hasty in thy spirit to be angry: for anger resteth in the bosom of fools. ECCLESIASTES 7:8–9

And so, after he had patiently endured, he obtained the promise.   HEBREWS 6:15

CHRIST ALONE
CAN BRING LASTING PEACE—
PEACE WITH GOD—
PEACE AMONG
MEN AND NATIONS—
AND PEACE
WITHIN OUR HEARTS.
Billy Graham

Blessed are the peacemakers: for they shall be called the children of God.　　　　　MATTHEW 5:9

Deceit is in the heart of them that imagine evil: but to the counsellors of peace is joy.　PROVERBS 12:20

And the fruit of righteousness is sown in peace of them that make peace.　　　　　JAMES 3:18

Endeavouring to keep the unity of the Spirit in the bond of peace.   EPHESIANS 4:3

Glory to God in the highest, and on earth peace, good will toward men.   LUKE 2:14

Flee also youthful lusts: but follow righteousness, faith, charity, peace, with them that call on the Lord out of a pure heart.   2 TIMOTHY 2:22

Mark the perfect man, and behold the upright: for the end of that man is peace.   PSALM 37:37

If it be possible, as much as lieth in you, live peaceably with all men.   ROMANS 12:18

And he shall judge among the nations, and shall rebuke many people: and they shall beat their swords into plowshares, and their spears into pruninghooks: nation shall not lift up sword against nation, neither shall they learn war any more.   ISAIAH 2:4

And the peace of God, which passeth all understanding, shall keep your hearts and minds through Christ Jesus.   PHILIPPIANS 4:7

And to esteem them very highly in love for their work's sake. And be at peace among yourselves.
                          1 THESSALONIANS 5:13

Behold, how good and how pleasant it is for brethren to dwell together in unity!   PSALM 133:1

I exhort therefore, that, first of all, supplications, prayers, intercessions, and giving of thanks, be made for all men;

For kings, and for all that are in authority; that we may lead a quiet and peaceable life in all godliness and honesty. 1 TIMOTHY 2:1–2

PEACE I LEAVE WITH YOU,
MY PEACE I GIVE
UNTO YOU:
NOT AS THE WORLD GIVETH,
GIVE I UNTO YOU.
LET NOT YOUR HEART
BE TROUBLED,
NEITHER LET IT BE AFRAID.
John 14:27

For God hath not given us the spirit of fear; but of power, and of love, and of a sound mind.

2 TIMOTHY 1:7

For he that will love life, and see good days, let him refrain his tongue from evil, and his lips that they speak no guile:

Let him eschew evil, and do good; let him seek peace, and ensue it. 1 PETER 3:10–11

Thou wilt keep him in perfect peace, whose mind is stayed on thee: because he trusteth in thee.

ISAIAH 26:3

REGARDLESS OF
WHAT YOU ARE DOING,
IF YOU PUMP LONG ENOUGH,
HARD ENOUGH AND
ENTHUSIASTICALLY ENOUGH,
SOONER OR LATER THE EFFORT
WILL BRING FORTH
THE REWARD.
Zig Ziglar

Let us hold fast the profession of our faith without wavering; (for he is faithful that promised).

HEBREWS 10:23

Stand fast therefore in the liberty wherewith Christ hath made us free, and be not entangled again with the yoke of bondage.   GALATIANS 5:1

For I am persuaded, that neither death, nor life, nor angels, nor principalities, nor powers, nor things present, nor things to come,

Nor height, nor depth, nor any other creature, shall be able to separate us from the love of God, which is in Christ Jesus our Lord.

ROMANS 8:38–39

But the path of the just is as the shining light, that shineth more and more unto the perfect day.

PROVERBS 4:18

To him that overcometh will I grant to sit with me in my throne, even as I also overcame, and am set down with my Father in his throne.

REVELATION 3:21

Then said Jesus to those Jews which believed on him, If ye continue in my word, then are ye my disciples indeed.

JOHN 8:31

Ye therefore, beloved, seeing ye know these things before, beware lest ye also, being led away with the error of the wicked, fall from your own stedfastness.

2 PETER 3:17

Confirming the souls of the disciples, and exhorting them to continue in the faith, and that we must through much tribulation enter into the kingdom of God.

ACTS 14:22

Who shall separate us from the love of Christ? shall tribulation, or distress, or persecution, or famine, or nakedness, or peril, or sword?   ROMANS 8:35

Wherefore take unto you the whole armour of God, that ye may be able to withstand in the evil day, and having done all, to stand.   EPHESIANS 6:13

THOUGH HE FALL,
HE SHALL NOT BE
UTTERLY CAST DOWN:
FOR THE LORD UPHOLDETH
HIM WITH HIS HAND.
Psalm 37:24

Wherefore seeing we also are compassed about with so great a cloud of witnesses, let us lay aside every weight, and the sin which doth so easily beset us, and let us run with patience the race that is set before us,

Looking unto Jesus the author and finisher of our faith; who for the joy that was set before him endured the cross, despising the shame, and is set down at the right hand of the throne of God.
          HEBREWS 12:1–2

Therefore, my brethren dearly beloved and longed for, my joy and crown, so stand fast in the Lord, my dearly beloved.   PHILIPPIANS 4:1

For the which cause I also suffer these things: nevertheless I am not ashamed: for I know whom I have believed, and am persuaded that he is able to keep that which I have committed unto him against that day.

Hold fast the form of sound words, which thou hast heard of me, in faith and love which is in Christ Jesus.   2 TIMOTHY 1:12–13

For now we live, if ye stand fast in the Lord.
                              1 THESSALONIANS 3:8

He that hath an ear, let him hear what the Spirit saith unto the churches; He that overcometh shall not be hurt of the second death.   REVELATION 2:11

For we are made partakers of Christ, if we hold the beginning of our confidence stedfast unto the end.
                                      HEBREWS 3:14

That the trial of your faith, being much more precious than of gold that perisheth, though it be tried with fire, might be found unto praise and honour and glory at the appearing of Jesus Christ.
                                        1 PETER 1:7

Praying always with all prayer and supplication in the Spirit, and watching thereunto with all perseverance and supplication for all saints.
                                    EPHESIANS 6:18

AN INFINITE GOD CAN
GIVE ALL OF HIMSELF TO
EACH OF HIS CHILDREN.
HE DOES NOT DISTRIBUTE HIMSELF
THAT EACH MAY HAVE A PART,
BUT TO EACH ONE HE GIVES
ALL OF HIMSELF
AS FULLY AS IF
THERE WERE NO OTHERS.

A. W. Tozer

Now unto him that is able to do exceeding abundantly above all that we ask or think, according to the power that worketh in us.   EPHESIANS 3:20

Seek the LORD and his strength, seek his face continually.   1 CHRONICLES 16:11

But ye shall receive power, after that the Holy Ghost is come upon you: and ye shall be witnesses unto me both in Jerusalem, and in all Judaea, and in Samaria, and unto the uttermost part of the earth.

ACTS 1:8

And what is the exceeding greatness of his power to us-ward who believe, according to the working of his mighty power,

Which he wrought in Christ, when he raised him from the dead, and set him at his own right hand in the heavenly places.   EPHESIANS 1:19–20

For our gospel came not unto you in word only, but also in power, and in the Holy Ghost, and in much assurance; as ye know what manner of men we were among you for your sake.   1 THESSALONIANS 1:5

The LORD thy God in the midst of thee is mighty; he will save, he will rejoice over thee with joy; he will rest in his love, he will joy over thee with singing.

ZEPHANIAH 3:17

FOR THE KINGDOM OF GOD IS NOT IN WORD, BUT IN POWER.
1 Corinthians 4:20

And have tasted the good word of God, and the powers of the world to come.   HEBREWS 6:5

PRAYER

> WORK AS IF
> YOU WERE TO LIVE
> A HUNDRED YEARS.
> PRAY AS IF
> YOU WERE TO DIE TOMORROW.
>
> *Benjamin Franklin*

But thou, when thou prayest, enter into thy closet, and when thou hast shut thy door, pray to thy Father which is in secret; and thy Father which seeth in secret shall reward thee openly.

But when ye pray, use not vain repetitions, as the heathen do: for they think that they shall be heard for their much speaking.   MATTHEW 6:6–7

But we will give ourselves continually to prayer, and to the ministry of the word.   ACTS 6:4

Give ear to my words, O LORD, consider my meditation.

Hearken unto the voice of my cry, my King, and my God: for unto thee will I pray.

My voice shalt thou hear in the morning, O LORD; in the morning will I direct my prayer unto thee, and will look up. PSALM 5:1–3

If ye then, being evil, know how to give good gifts unto your children, how much more shall your Father which is in heaven give good things to them that ask him? MATTHEW 7:11

Rejoicing in hope; patient in tribulation; continuing instant in prayer. ROMANS 12:12

Evening, and morning, and at noon, will I pray, and cry aloud: and he shall hear my voice.
PSALM 55:17

He shall call upon me, and I will answer him.
PSALM 91:15

He will be very gracious unto thee at the voice of thy cry; when he shall hear it, he will answer thee.
ISAIAH 30:19

Thou shalt make thy prayer unto him, and he shall hear thee, and thou shalt pay thy vows. JOB 22:27

I waited patiently for the LORD; and he inclined unto me, and heard my cry. PSALM 40:1

Praying always with all prayer and supplication in the Spirit, and watching thereunto with all perseverance and supplication for all saints.

EPHESIANS 6:18

PRAY WITHOUT CEASING.
1 Thessalonians 5:17

And shall not God avenge his own elect, which cry day and night unto him, though he bear long with them? LUKE 18:7

If my people, which are called by my name, shall humble themselves, and pray, and seek my face, and turn from their wicked ways; then will I hear from heaven, and will forgive their sin, and will heal their land. 2 CHRONICLES 7:14

Then shall ye call upon me, and ye shall go and pray unto me, and I will hearken unto you.

JEREMIAH 29:12

And all things, whatsoever ye shall ask in prayer, believing, ye shall receive. MATTHEW 21:22

The LORD is nigh unto all them that call upon him, to all that call upon him in truth. PSALM 145:18

Because he hath inclined his ear unto me, therefore will I call upon him as long as I live. PSALM 116:2

Let us therefore come boldly unto the throne of grace, that we may obtain mercy, and find grace to help in time of need.   HEBREWS 4:16

The sacrifice of the wicked is an abomination to the LORD: but the prayer of the upright is his delight.
                                   PROVERBS 15:8

Ask, and it shall be given you; seek, and ye shall find; knock, and it shall be opened unto you:
    For every one that asketh receiveth; and he that seeketh findeth; and to him that knocketh it shall be opened.   MATTHEW 7:7–8

Confess your faults one to another, and pray one for another, that ye may be healed. The effectual fervent prayer of a righteous man availeth much.
                                   JAMES 5:16

And this is the confidence that we have in him, that, if we ask any thing according to his will, he heareth us:
    And if we know that he hear us, whatsoever we ask, we know that we have the petitions that we desired of him.   1 JOHN 5:14–15

And it shall come to pass, that before they call, I will answer; and while they are yet speaking, I will hear.
                                   ISAIAH 65:24

Be not wise in thine own eyes: fear the LORD, and depart from evil.   PROVERBS 3:7

Likewise the Spirit also helpeth our infirmities: for we know not what we should pray for as we ought: but the Spirit itself maketh intercession for us with groanings which cannot be uttered. ROMANS 8:26

Oh that men would praise the LORD for his goodness, and for his wonderful works to the children of men! PSALM 107:15

SO THAT THEY CAUSE
THE CRY OF THE POOR
TO COME UNTO HIM,
AND HE HEARETH
THE CRY OF THE AFFLICTED.
Job 34:28

I will pray with the spirit, and I will pray with the understanding also: I will sing with the spirit, and I will sing with the understanding also.
1 CORINTHIANS 14:15

Yet the LORD will command his lovingkindness in the daytime, and in the night his song shall be with me, and my prayer unto the God of my life.
PSALM 42:8

PRIDE IS SELDOM DELICATE;
IT WILL PLEASE ITSELF
WITH VERY MEAN ADVANTAGES.
Samuel Johnson

And he sat down, and called the twelve, and saith unto them, If any man desire to be first, the same shall be last of all, and servant of all.   MARK 9:35

Surely God will not hear vanity, neither will the Almighty regard it.   JOB 35:13

An high look, and a proud heart, and the plowing of the wicked, is sin.   PROVERBS 21:4

But now ye rejoice in your boastings: all such rejoicing is evil.   JAMES 4:16

Be of the same mind one toward another. Mind not high things, but condescend to men of low estate. Be not wise in your own conceits.   ROMANS 12:16

WHICH RECEIVE HONOUR ONE OF ANOTHER, AND SEEK NOT THE HONOUR THAT COMETH FROM GOD ONLY?
John 5:44

Woe unto them that are wise in their own eyes, and prudent in their own sight!   ISAIAH 5:21

Talk no more so exceeding proudly; let not arrogancy come out of your mouth: for the LORD is a God of knowledge, and by him actions are weighed.
1 SAMUEL 2:3

The fear of the LORD is to hate evil: pride, and arrogancy, and the evil way, and the froward mouth, do I hate.   PROVERBS 8:13

And he said unto them, Ye are they which justify yourselves before men; but God knoweth your hearts: for that which is highly esteemed among men is abomination in the sight of God.   LUKE 16:15

Pride goeth before destruction, and an haughty spirit before a fall.   PROVERBS 16:18

He that is of a proud heart stirreth up strife: but he that putteth his trust in the LORD shall be made fat.

He that trusteth in his own heart is a fool: but whoso walketh wisely, he shall be delivered.

PROVERBS 28:25–26

Let not the foot of pride come against me, and let not the hand of the wicked remove me.

PSALM 36:11

For I say, through the grace given unto me, to every man that is among you, not to think of himself more highly than he ought to think; but to think soberly, according as God hath dealt to every man the measure of faith. ROMANS 12:3

WHEN PRIDE COMETH,
THEN COMETH SHAME:
BUT WITH THE LOWLY
IS WISDOM.
Proverbs 11:2

But he that glorieth, let him glory in the Lord.

For not he that commendeth himself is approved, but whom the Lord commendeth.

2 CORINTHIANS 10:17–18

For if a man think himself to be something, when he is nothing, he deceiveth himself. GALATIANS 6:3

GOD BRINGS MEN
INTO DEEP WATERS
NOT TO DROWN THEM,
BUT TO CLEANSE THEM.

John H. Aughey

Be thou my strong habitation, whereunto I may continually resort: thou hast given commandment to save me, for thou art my rock and my fortress.

PSALM 71:3

Above all, taking the shield of faith, wherewith ye shall be able to quench all the fiery darts of the wicked.

EPHESIANS 6:16

Our soul waiteth for the LORD: he is our help and our shield.

PSALM 33:20

For thou, Lord, wilt bless the righteous; with favour wilt thou compass him as with a shield.

PSALM 5:12

The LORD liveth; and blessed be my rock; and exalted be the God of the rock of my salvation.

2 SAMUEL 22:47

Thou hast also given me the shield of thy salvation: and thy right hand hath holden me up, and thy gentleness hath made me great.   PSALM 18:35

The name of the LORD is a strong tower: the righteous runneth into it, and is safe.   PROVERBS 18:10

Every word of God is pure: he is a shield unto them that put their trust in him.   PROVERBS 30:5

For thou art my rock and my fortress; therefore for thy name's sake lead me, and guide me.

PSALM 31:3

He shall cover thee with his feathers, and under his wings shalt thou trust: his truth shall be thy shield and buckler.   PSALM 91:4

But whoso hearkeneth unto me shall dwell safely, and shall be quiet from fear of evil.

PROVERBS 1:33

And he said, The LORD is my rock, and my fortress, and my deliverer;

The God of my rock; in him will I trust: he is my shield, and the horn of my salvation, my high tower, and my refuge, my saviour; thou savest me from violence.

I will call on the LORD, who is worthy to be praised: so shall I be saved from mine enemies.

2 SAMUEL 22:2–4

The LORD is good, a strong hold in the day of trouble; and he knoweth them that trust in him.

NAHUM 1:7

The LORD is my rock, and my fortress, and my deliverer; my God, my strength, in whom I will trust; my buckler, and the horn of my salvation, and my high tower.

PSALM 18:2

God is our refuge and strength, a very present help in trouble.

Therefore will not we fear, though the earth be removed, and though the mountains be carried into the midst of the sea;

Though the waters thereof roar and be troubled, though the mountains shake with the swelling thereof. Selah.

PSALM 46:1–3

Cast thy burden upon the LORD, and he shall sustain thee: he shall never suffer the righteous to be moved.

PSALM 55:22

The eternal God is thy refuge, and underneath are the everlasting arms.   DEUTERONOMY 33:27

The LORD also will be a refuge for the oppressed, a refuge in times of trouble.   PSALM 9:9

> GOD IS OUR REFUGE
> AND STRENGTH,
> A VERY PRESENT HELP
> IN TROUBLE.
> *Psalm 46:1*

That by two immutable things, in which it was impossible for God to lie, we might have a strong consolation, who have fled for refuge to lay hold upon the hope set before us.   HEBREWS 6:18

The LORD of hosts is with us; the God of Jacob is our refuge. Selah.   PSALM 46:7

But the LORD is my defence; and my God is the rock of my refuge.   PSALM 94:22

In the fear of the LORD is strong confidence: and his children shall have a place of refuge.
    PROVERBS 14:26

PURITY

NO ONE CAN MAKE HIMSELF
PURE BY OBEYING LAWS.
JESUS CHRIST DOES NOT GIVE US
RULES AND REGULATIONS—
HE GIVES US HIS TEACHINGS
WHICH ARE TRUTHS THAT CAN
ONLY BE INTERPRETED BY
HIS NATURE WHICH
HE PLACES WITHIN US.

Oswald Chambers

But I say unto you, That whosoever looketh on a woman to lust after her hath committed adultery with her already in his heart.   MATTHEW 5:28

Drink waters out of thine own cistern, and running waters out of thine own well.   PROVERBS 5:15

To keep thee from the evil woman, from the flattery of the tongue of a strange woman.

Lust not after her beauty in thine heart; neither let her take thee with her eyelids.

For by means of a whorish woman a man is brought to a piece of bread: and the adulteress will hunt for the precious life.

Can a man take fire in his bosom, and his clothes not be burned?

Can one go upon hot coals, and his feet not be burned?

So he that goeth in to his neighbour's wife; whosoever toucheth her shall not be innocent.

PROVERBS 6:24–29

But fornication, and all uncleanness, or covetousness, let it not be once named among you, as becometh saints.　　　EPHESIANS 5:3

Thou shalt not commit adultery.　　EXODUS 20:14

Mortify therefore your members which are upon the earth; fornication, uncleanness, inordinate affection, evil concupiscence, and covetousness, which is idolatry:

For which things' sake the wrath of God cometh on the children of disobedience.

COLOSSIANS 3:5–6

I MADE A COVENANT
WITH MINE EYES;
WHY THEN SHOULD
I THINK UPON A MAID?
Job 31:1

Meats for the belly, and the belly for meats: but God shall destroy both it and them. Now the body is not for fornication, but for the Lord; and the Lord for the body.

And God hath both raised up the Lord, and will also raise up us by his own power.

Know ye not that your bodies are the members of Christ? shall I then take the members of Christ, and make them the members of an harlot? God forbid.

What? know ye not that he which is joined to an harlot is one body? for two, saith he, shall be one flesh.

But he that is joined unto the Lord is one spirit.

Flee fornication. Every sin that a man doeth is without the body; but he that committeth fornication sinneth against his own body.

What? know ye not that your body is the temple of the Holy Ghost which is in you, which ye have of God, and ye are not your own?

For ye are bought with a price: therefore glorify God in your body, and in your spirit, which are God's.   1 CORINTHIANS 6:13–20

REPENTANCE IS A CHANGE OF WILLING, OF FEELING, AND OF LIVING, IN RESPECT TO GOD.

Charles Finney

Repent ye therefore, and be converted, that your sins may be blotted out, when the times of refreshing shall come from the presence of the Lord.

ACTS 3:19

I will have mercy, and not sacrifice: for I am not come to call the righteous, but sinners to repentance.

MATTHEW 9:13

Likewise, I say unto you, there is joy in the presence of the angels of God over one sinner that repenteth.

LUKE 15:10

The time is fulfilled, and the kingdom of God is at hand: repent ye, and believe the gospel.

MARK 1:15

He looketh upon men, and if any say, I have sinned, and perverted that which was right, and it profited me not;

He will deliver his soul from going into the pit, and his life shall see the light. JOB 33:27–28

And the times of this ignorance God winked at; but now commandeth all men every where to repent.

ACTS 17:30

Remember therefore how thou hast received and heard, and hold fast, and repent. If therefore thou shalt not watch, I will come on thee as a thief, and thou shalt not know what hour I will come upon thee. REVELATION 3:3

He that covereth his sins shall not prosper: but whoso confesseth and forsaketh them shall have mercy. PROVERBS 28:13

Or despisest thou the riches of his goodness and forbearance and longsuffering; not knowing that the goodness of God leadeth thee to repentance?

ROMANS 2:4

Turn unto the LORD your God: for he is gracious and merciful, slow to anger, and of great kindness, and repenteth him of the evil. JOEL 2:13

Seek ye the LORD while he may be found, call ye upon him while he is near:

Let the wicked forsake his way, and the unrighteous man his thoughts: and let him return unto the LORD, and he will have mercy upon him; and to our God, for he will abundantly pardon.

ISAIAH 55:6–7

AND SAYING,
THE TIME IS FULFILLED,
AND THE KINGDOM OF GOD
IS AT HAND: REPENT YE,
AND BELIEVE THE GOSPEL.

Mark 1:15

The LORD is nigh unto them that are of a broken heart; and saveth such as be of a contrite spirit.

PSALM 34:18

REPUTATION

**IF YOU ARE GOING TO
MAKE A DIFFERENCE,
YOU MIGHT AS WELL MAKE IT
A POSITIVE ONE.**
Cal Ripken, Jr.

Neither do men light a candle, and put it under a bushel, but on a candlestick; and it giveth light unto all that are in the house.

Let your light so shine before men, that they may see your good works, and glorify your Father which is in heaven.   MATTHEW 5:15–16

Every man's work shall be made manifest: for the day shall declare it, because it shall be revealed by fire; and the fire shall try every man's work of what sort it is.   1 CORINTHIANS 3:13

A good name is rather to be chosen than great riches, and loving favour rather than silver and gold.

PROVERBS 22:1

But he that doeth truth cometh to the light, that his deeds may be made manifest, that they are wrought in God.

JOHN 3:21

Blessed is the man that walketh not in the counsel of the ungodly, nor standeth in the way of sinners, nor sitteth in the seat of the scornful.

PSALM 1:1

Ye shall know them by their fruits. Do men gather grapes of thorns, or figs of thistles?

Even so every good tree bringeth forth good fruit; but a corrupt tree bringeth forth evil fruit.

A good tree cannot bring forth evil fruit, neither can a corrupt tree bring forth good fruit.

Every tree that bringeth not forth good fruit is hewn down, and cast into the fire.

Wherefore by their fruits ye shall know them.

MATTHEW 7:16–20

Therefore, seeing we have this ministry, as we have received mercy, we faint not;

But have renounced the hidden things of dishonesty, not walking in craftiness, nor handling the word of God deceitfully; but by manifestation of the truth commending ourselves to every man's conscience in the sight of God.

2 CORINTHIANS 4:1–2

Now therefore ye are no more strangers and foreigners, but fellowcitizens with the saints, and of the household of God;

And are built upon the foundation of the apostles and prophets, Jesus Christ himself being the chief corner stone. EPHESIANS 2:19–20

A GOOD NAME IS BETTER
THAN PRECIOUS OINTMENT;
AND THE DAY OF DEATH
THAN THE DAY OF
ONE'S BIRTH.
Ecclesiastes 7:1

RESPONSIBILITY IS
THE PRICE OF GREATNESS.
Winston Churchill

Now he that planteth and he that watereth are one: and every man shall receive his own reward according to his own labour. 1 CORINTHIANS 3:8

The soul that sinneth, it shall die. The son shall not bear the iniquity of the father, neither shall the father bear the iniquity of the son: the righteousness of the righteous shall be upon him, and the wickedness of the wicked shall be upon him.

EZEKIEL 18:20

For by thy words thou shalt be justified, and by thy words thou shalt be condemned. MATTHEW 12:37

I am he which searcheth the reins and hearts: and I will give unto every one of you according to your works.   REVELATION 2:23

And he said, Now also let it be according unto your words: he with whom it is found shall be my servant; and ye shall be blameless.   GENESIS 44:10

That ye may be blameless and harmless, the sons of God, without rebuke, in the midst of a crooked and perverse nation, among whom ye shine as lights in the world.   PHILIPPIANS 2:15

Dearly beloved, I beseech you as strangers and pilgrims, abstain from fleshly lusts, which war against the soul;

Having your conversation honest among the Gentiles: that, whereas they speak against you as evildoers, they may by your good works, which they shall behold, glorify God in the day of visitation.

Submit yourselves to every ordinance of man for the Lord's sake: whether it be to the king, as supreme;

Or unto governors, as unto them that are sent by him for the punishment of evildoers, and for the praise of them that do well.

For so is the will of God, that with well doing ye may put to silence the ignorance of foolish men:

As free, and not using your liberty for a cloke of maliciousness, but as the servants of God.
    1 PETER 2:11–16

And they were both righteous before God, walking in all the commandments and ordinances of the Lord blameless. LUKE 1:6

FOR EVERY MAN SHALL BEAR HIS OWN BURDEN.
Galatians 6:5

Therefore I will judge you, O house of Israel, every one according to his ways, saith the Lord GOD. Repent, and turn yourselves from all your transgressions; so iniquity shall not be your ruin.

EZEKIEL 18:30

REST

EVERY NOW AND THEN GO AWAY,
HAVE A LITTLE RELAXATION,
FOR WHEN YOU COME BACK
TO YOUR WORK YOUR JUDGMENT
WILL BE SURER.

Leonardo Da Vinci

And thou shalt be secure, because there is hope; yea, thou shalt dig about thee, and thou shalt take thy rest in safety. JOB 11:18

When thou liest down, thou shalt not be afraid: yea, thou shalt lie down, and thy sleep shall be sweet. PROVERBS 3:24

Six days may work be done; but in the seventh is the sabbath of rest, holy to the LORD. EXODUS 31:15

It is vain for you to rise up early, to sit up late, to eat the bread of sorrows: for so he giveth his beloved sleep.   PSALM 127:2

For he spake in a certain place of the seventh day on this wise, And God did rest the seventh day from all his works. . . .

There remaineth therefore a rest to the people of God.   HEBREWS 4:4, 9

He that dwelleth in the secret place of the most High shall abide under the shadow of the Almighty.
                                                                   PSALM 91:1

RIGHTEOUSNESS

THE MAN OF LIFE UPRIGHT,
WHOSE GUILTLESS HEART IS FREE
FROM ALL DISHONEST DEEDS
OR THOUGHT OF VANITY. . .
Thomas Campion

Thy word is true from the beginning: and every one of thy righteous judgments endureth for ever.

PSALM 119:160

Then shall the righteous shine forth as the sun in the kingdom of their Father. Who hath ears to hear, let him hear.

MATTHEW 13:43

The righteous cry, and the LORD heareth, and delivereth them out of all their troubles.

PSALM 34:17

Whereby are given unto us exceeding great and precious promises: that by these ye might be partakers of the divine nature, having escaped the corruption that is in the world through lust.   2 PETER 1:4

But if thou shalt indeed obey his voice, and do all that I speak; then I will be an enemy unto thine enemies, and an adversary unto thine adversaries.
EXODUS 23:22

If we confess our sins, he is faithful and just to fogive us our sins, and to cleanse us from all unrighteousness.   1 JOHN 1:9

Ye that love the LORD, hate evil: he preserveth the souls of his saints; he delivereth them out of the hand of the wicked.

Light is sown for the righteous.
PSALM 97:10–11

And it shall come to pass, if thou shalt hearken diligently unto the voice of the LORD thy God, to observe and to do all his commandments which I command thee this day, that the LORD thy God will set thee on high above all nations of the earth.
DEUTERONOMY 28:1

He withdraweth not his eyes from the righteous: but with kings are they on the throne; yea, he doth establish them for ever, and they are exalted.
JOB 36:7

The eyes of the LORD are upon the righteous, and his ears are open unto their cry.   PSALM 34:15

The LORD will not suffer the soul of the righteous to famish: but he casteth away the substance of the wicked.   PROVERBS 10:3

Then shall thy light break forth as the morning, and thine health shall spring forth speedily: and thy righteousness shall go before thee; the glory of the LORD shall be thy rereward.   ISAIAH 58:8

But know that the LORD hath set apart him that is godly for himself: the LORD will hear when I call unto him.   PSALM 4:3

Then shall he answer them, saying, Verily I say unto you, Inasmuch as ye did it not to one of the least of these, ye did it not to me.
    And these shall go away into everlasting punishment: but the righteous into life eternal.
          MATTHEW 25:45–46

He that followeth after righteousness and mercy findeth life, righteousness, and honour.
          PROVERBS 21:21

The righteous shall be glad in the LORD, and shall trust in him; and all the upright in heart shall glory.
          PSALM 64:10

Blessed are they which do hunger and thirst after righteousness: for they shall be filled.

MATTHEW 5:6

A righteous man hateth lying: but a wicked man is loathsome, and cometh to shame.   PROVERBS 13:5

BLESSED ARE THEY
WHICH ARE PERSECUTED
FOR RIGHTEOUSNESS'
SAKE: FOR THEIRS IS THE
KINGDOM OF HEAVEN.
Matthew 5:10

Know ye not that the unrighteous shall not inherit the kingdom of God? Be not deceived.

1 CORINTHIANS 6:9

LORD, who shall abide in thy tabernacle? who shall dwell in thy holy hill?

He that walketh uprightly, and worketh righteousness, and speaketh the truth in his heart.

PSALM 15:1–2

PERSONAL SALVATION IS NOT
AN OCCASIONAL RENDEZVOUS
WITH GOD.
CHRISTIANITY IS NOT JUST
AN AVOCATION;
IT IS A LIFELONG,
ETERNITY-LONG VOCATION.

Billy Graham

But after that the kindness and love of God our Saviour toward man appeared,

Not by works of righteousness which we have done, but according to his mercy he saved us, by the washing of regeneration, and renewing of the Holy Ghost;

Which he shed on us abundantly through Jesus Christ our Saviour. TITUS 3:4–6

But as many as received him, to them gave he power to become the sons of God, even to them that believe on his name:

Which were born, not of blood, nor of the will of the flesh, nor of the will of man, but of God.

JOHN 1:12–13

Neither is there salvation in any other: for there is none other name under heaven given among men, whereby we must be saved. ACTS 4:12

For he hath made him to be sin for us, who knew no sin; that we might be made the righteousness of God in him. 2 CORINTHIANS 5:21

Even as I please all men in all things, not seeking mine own profit, but the profit of many, that they may be saved. 1 CORINTHIANS 10:33

Jesus answered and said unto him, Verily, verily, I say unto thee, Except a man be born again, he cannot see the kingdom of God.

Nicodemus saith unto him, How can a man be born when he is old? can he enter the second time into his mother's womb, and be born?

Jesus answered, Verily, verily, I say unto thee, Except a man be born of water and of the Spirit, he cannot enter into the kingdom of God.

That which is born of the flesh is flesh; and that which is born of the Spirit is spirit.

Marvel not that I said unto thee, Ye must be born again. JOHN 3:3–7

Therefore if any man be in Christ, he is a new creature: old things are passed away; behold, all things are become new.   2 CORINTHIANS 5:17

HE THAT BELIEVETH ON THE SON HATH EVERLASTING LIFE.
John 3:36

My little children, these things write I unto you, that ye sin not. And if any man sin, we have an advocate with the Father, Jesus Christ the righteous:

And he is the propitiation for our sins: and not for ours only, but also for the sins of the whole world.
1 JOHN 2:1–2

For this is good and acceptable in the sight of God our Saviour;

Who will have all men to be saved, and to come unto the knowledge of the truth.
1 TIMOTHY 2:3–4

GOD DID NOT WRITE A BOOK
AND SEND IT BY MESSENGER
TO BE READ AT A DISTANCE
BY UNAIDED MINDS.
HE SPOKE A BOOK AND
LIVES IN HIS SPOKEN WORDS,
CONSTANTLY SPEAKING HIS WORDS
AND CAUSING THE POWER
OF THEM TO PERSIST
ACROSS THE YEARS.

A. W. Tozer

That ye may be mindful of the words which were spoken before by the holy prophets, and of the commandment of us the apostles of the Lord and Saviour. 2 PETER 3:2

So shall my word be that goeth forth out of my mouth: it shall not return unto me void, but it shall accomplish that which I please, and it shall prosper in the thing whereto I sent it.   ISAIAH 55:11

Thy word have I hid in mine heart, that I might not sin against thee.   PSALM 119:11

God, who at sundry times and in divers manners spake in time past unto the fathers by the prophets,
     Hath in these last days spoken unto us by his Son, whom he hath appointed heir of all things, by whom also he made the worlds.   HEBREWS 1:1–2

This book of the law shall not depart out of thy mouth; but thou shalt meditate therein day and night, that thou mayest observe to do according to all that is written therein: for then thou shalt make thy way prosperous, and then thou shalt have good success.
          JOSHUA 1:8

Searching what, or what manner of time the Spirit of Christ which was in them did signify, when it testified beforehand the sufferings of Christ, and the glory that should follow.
     Unto whom it was revealed, that not unto themselves, but unto us they did minister the things, which are now reported unto you by them that have preached the gospel unto you with the Holy Ghost sent down from heaven; which things the angels desire to look into.   1 PETER 1:11–12

Let the word of Christ dwell in you richly in all wisdom; teaching and admonishing one another in psalms and hymns and spiritual songs, singing with grace in your hearts to the Lord.   COLOSSIANS 3:16

And that from a child thou hast known the holy scriptures, which are able to make thee wise unto salvation through faith which is in Christ Jesus.
2 TIMOTHY 3:15

THY WORD IS A LAMP
UNTO MY FEET,
AND A LIGHT
UNTO MY PATH.
Psalm 119:105

Therefore shall ye lay up these my words in your heart and in your soul, and bind them for a sign upon your hand, that they may be as frontlets between your eyes.

And ye shall teach them your children, speaking of them when thou sittest in thine house, and when thou walkest by the way, when thou liest down, and when thou risest up.   DEUTERONOMY 11:18–19

For the word of God is quick, and powerful, and sharper than any twoedged sword, piercing even to the dividing asunder of soul and spirit, and of the joints and marrow, and is a discerner of the thoughts and intents of the heart.   HEBREWS 4:12

SEEKING GOD

DON'T THINK SO MUCH ABOUT
WHO IS FOR OR AGAINST YOU,
RATHER GIVE ALL YOUR CARE,
THAT GOD BE WITH YOU
IN EVERYTHING YOU DO.

Thomas a Kempis

One thing have I desired of the LORD, that will I seek after; that I may dwell in the house of the LORD all the days of my life, to behold the beauty of the LORD, and to enquire in his temple.

PSALM 27:4

With my soul have I desired thee in the night; yea, with my spirit within me will I seek thee early: for when thy judgments are in the earth, the inhabitants of the world will learn righteousness.   ISAIAH 26:9

And ye shall seek me, and find me, when ye shall search for me with all your heart.   JEREMIAH 29:13

But seek ye first the kingdom of God, and his righteousness; and all these things shall be added unto you.   MATTHEW 6:33

Sow to yourselves in righteousness, reap in mercy; break up your fallow ground: for it is time to seek the LORD, till he come and rain righteousness upon you.   HOSEA 10:12

Seek the LORD and his strength, seek his face continually.   1 CHRONICLES 16:11

And I say unto you, Ask, and it shall be given you; seek, and ye shall find; knock, and it shall be opened unto you.   LUKE 11:9

SEEK THE LORD, AND YE SHALL LIVE.
Amos 5:6

Therefore came I forth to meet thee, diligently to seek thy face, and I have found thee.

PROVERBS 7:15

But if from thence thou shalt seek the LORD thy God, thou shalt find him, if thou seek him with all thy heart and with all thy soul.

DEUTERONOMY 4:29

If ye then be risen with Christ, seek those things which are above, where Christ sitteth on the right hand of God.   COLOSSIANS 3:1

THEY THAT SEEK
THE LORD SHALL NOT
WANT ANY GOOD THING.
Psalm 34:10

Glory ye in his holy name: let the heart of them rejoice that seek the LORD.   1 CHRONICLES 16:10

If my people, which are called by my name, shall humble themselves, and pray, and seek my face, and turn from their wicked ways; then will I hear from heaven, and will forgive their sin, and will heal their land.   2 CHRONICLES 7:14

HE WHO REIGNS
WITHIN HIMSELF
AND RULES PASSIONS,
DESIRES, AND FEARS IS
MORE THAN A KING.

John Milton

Then said Pilate unto him, Hearest thou not how many things they witness against thee?

And he answered him to never a word; insomuch that the governor marvelled greatly.

MATTHEW 27:13–14

If the spirit of the ruler rise up against thee, leave not thy place; for yielding pacifieth great offences.

ECCLESIASTES 10:4

For even hereunto were ye called: because Christ also suffered for us, leaving us an example, that ye should follow his steps:

Who did no sin, neither was guile found in his mouth:

Who, when he was reviled, reviled not again; when he suffered, he threatened not; but committed himself to him that judgeth righteously.

1 PETER 2:21–23

Charity suffereth long, and is kind; charity envieth not; charity vaunteth not itself, is not puffed up,

Doth not behave itself unseemly, seeketh not her own, is not easily provoked, thinketh no evil.

1 CORINTHIANS 13:4–5

Yet Michael the archangel, when contending with the devil he disputed about the body of Moses, durst not bring against him a railing accusation, but said, The Lord rebuke thee.

JUDE 9

Let us walk honestly, as in the day; not in rioting and drunkenness, not in chambering and wantonness, not in strife and envying.

But put ye on the Lord Jesus Christ, and make not provision for the flesh, to fulfil the lusts thereof.

ROMANS 13:13–14

Hast thou found honey? eat so much as is sufficient for thee, lest thou be filled therewith, and vomit it.

PROVERBS 25:16

Let your moderation be known unto all men. The Lord is at hand.   PHILIPPIANS 4:5

Therefore let us not sleep, as do others; but let us watch and be sober.

For they that sleep sleep in the night; and they that be drunken are drunken in the night.
                    1 THESSALONIANS 5:6–7

And beside this, giving all diligence, add to your faith virtue; and to virtue knowledge;

And to knowledge temperance; and to temperance patience; and to patience godliness.
                    2 PETER 1:5–6

And every man that striveth for the mastery is temperate in all things. Now they do it to obtain a corruptible crown; but we an incorruptible.
                    1 CORINTHIANS 9:25

For if ye live after the flesh, ye shall die: but if ye through the Spirit do mortify the deeds of the body, ye shall live.   ROMANS 8:13

Teaching us that, denying ungodliness and worldly lusts, we should live soberly, righteously, and godly, in this present world.   TITUS 2:12

But I keep under my body, and bring it into subjection: lest that by any means, when I have preached to others, I myself should be a castaway.
                    1 CORINTHIANS 9:27

He sitteth alone and keepeth silence, because he hath borne it upon him.

He putteth his mouth in the dust; if so be there may be hope.   LAMENTATIONS 3:28–29

BE GRAVE,
NOT DOUBLETONGUED,
NOT GIVEN TO MUCH WINE,
NOT GREEDY
OF FILTHY LUCRE.
1 Timothy 3:8

Neither fornicators, nor idolaters, nor adulterers, nor effeminate, nor abusers of themselves with mankind,

Nor thieves, nor covetous, nor drunkards, nor revilers, nor extortioners, shall inherit the kingdom of God.

And such were some of you: but ye are washed, but ye are sanctified, but ye are justified in the name of the Lord Jesus, and by the Spirit of our God.
                    1 CORINTHIANS 6:9–11

GIVE UP ALL OF SELF AND ITS LIFE,
AND DWELL IN GOD'S WILL
AND REST IN HIS STRENGTH.
THIS IS WHAT BRINGS
THE POWER THAT DOES NOT
COMMIT SIN.
Andrew Murray

Again, the kingdom of heaven is like unto a merchant man, seeking goodly pearls:

Who, when he had found one pearl of great price, went and sold all that he had, and bought it.
MATTHEW 13:45–46

We then that are strong ought to bear the infirmities of the weak, and not to please ourselves.
ROMANS 15:1

And he said to them all, If any man will come after me, let him deny himself, and take up his cross daily, and follow me.

For whosoever will save his life shall lose it: but whosoever will lose his life for my sake, the same shall save it. LUKE 9:23–24

But God forbid that I should glory, save in the cross of our Lord Jesus Christ, by whom the world is crucified unto me, and I unto the world.
GALATIANS 6:14

He that loveth his life shall lose it; and he that hateth his life in this world shall keep it unto life eternal. JOHN 12:25

And he said unto them, Verily I say unto you, There is no man that hath left house, or parents, or brethren, or wife, or children, for the kingdom of God's sake,

Who shall not receive manifold more in this present time, and in the world to come life everlasting.
LUKE 18:29–30

But what things were gain to me, those I counted loss for Christ.

Yea doubtless, and I count all things but loss for the excellency of the knowledge of Christ Jesus my Lord: for whom I have suffered the loss of all things, and do count them but dung, that I may win Christ. PHILIPPIANS 3:7–8

And if thy hand offend thee, cut it off: it is better for thee to enter into life maimed, than having two hands to go into hell, into the fire that never shall be quenched. MARK 9:43

If others be partakers of this power over you, are not we rather? Nevertheless we have not used this power; but suffer all things, lest we should hinder the gospel of Christ. 1 CORINTHIANS 9:12

I am crucified with Christ: nevertheless I live; yet not I, but Christ liveth in me: and the life which I now live in the flesh I live by the faith of the Son of God, who loved me, and gave himself for me.
GALATIANS 2:20

AND WHOSOEVER DOTH
NOT BEAR HIS CROSS,
AND COME AFTER ME,
CANNOT BE MY DISCIPLE.
Luke 14:27

No man that warreth entangleth himself with the affairs of this life; that he may please him who hath chosen him to be a soldier. 2 TIMOTHY 2:4

Blessed is the man that endureth temptation: for when he is tried, he shall receive the crown of life, which the Lord hath promised to them that love him.
JAMES 1:12

Forasmuch then as Christ hath suffered for us in the flesh, arm yourselves likewise with the same mind: for he that hath suffered in the flesh hath ceased from sin;

That he no longer should live the rest of his time in the flesh to the lusts of men, but to the will of God.   1 PETER 4:1–2

And a certain scribe came, and said unto him, Master, I will follow thee whithersoever thou goest.

And Jesus saith unto him, The foxes have holes, and the birds of the air have nests; but the Son of man hath not where to lay his head.

MATTHEW 8:19–20

This I say then, Walk in the Spirit, and ye shall not fulfil the lust of the flesh.

For the flesh lusteth against the Spirit, and the Spirit against the flesh: and these are contrary the one to the other: so that ye cannot do the things that ye would.   GALATIANS 5:16–17

SIN PAYS—
BUT IT PAYS OFF IN REMORSE,
REGRET, AND FAILURE.
Billy Graham

Come now, and let us reason together, saith the LORD: though your sins be as scarlet, they shall be as white as snow; though they be red like crimson, they shall be as wool.   ISAIAH 1:18

For this is my blood of the new testament, which is shed for many for the remission of sins.
                                        MATTHEW 26:28

Therefore if any man be in Christ, he is a new creature: old things are passed away; behold, all things are become new.   2 CORINTHIANS 5:17

My little children, these things write I unto you, that ye sin not. And if any man sin, we have an advocate with the Father, Jesus Christ the righteous:

And he is the propitiation for our sins: and not for ours only, but also for the sins of the whole world.
1 JOHN 2:1–2

But if we walk in the light, as he is in the light, we have fellowship one with another, and the blood of Jesus Christ his Son cleanseth us from all sin.
1 JOHN 1:7

To him give all the prophets witness, that through his name whosoever believeth in him shall receive remission of sins.
ACTS 10:43

Who his own self bare our sins in his own body on the tree, that we, being dead to sins, should live unto righteousness: by whose stripes ye were healed.
1 PETER 2:24

Who gave himself for our sins, that he might deliver us from this present evil world, according to the will of God and our Father.
GALATIANS 1:4

But he was wounded for our transgressions, he was bruised for our iniquities: the chastisement of our peace was upon him; and with his stripes we are healed.

All we like sheep have gone astray; we have turned every one to his own way; and the LORD hath laid on him the iniquity of us all.
ISAIAH 53:5–6

Knowing this, that our old man is crucified with him, that the body of sin might be destroyed, that henceforth we should not serve sin.

For he that is dead is freed from sin.

ROMANS 6:6–7

FOR I WILL BE
MERCIFUL TO THEIR
UNRIGHTEOUSNESS,
AND THEIR SINS AND
THEIR INIQUITIES WILL
I REMEMBER NO MORE.
Hebrews 8:12

This is a faithful saying, and worthy of all acceptation, that Christ Jesus came into the world to save sinners; of whom I am chief.   1 TIMOTHY 1:15

SINCERITY

SINCERITY MAKES
THE VERY LEAST PERSON
TO BE OF MORE VALUE THAN
THE MOST TALENTED HYPOCRITE.
Charles H. Spurgeon

As newborn babes, desire the sincere milk of the word, that ye may grow thereby.   1 PETER 2:2

For we are not as many, which corrupt the word of God: but as of sincerity, but as of God, in the sight of God speak we in Christ.   2 CORINTHIANS 2:17

Now therefore fear the LORD, and serve him in sincerity and in truth.   JOSHUA 24:14

Now the end of the commandment is charity out of a pure heart, and of a good conscience, and of faith unfeigned. 1 TIMOTHY 1:5

Seeing ye have purified your souls in obeying the truth through the Spirit unto unfeigned love of the brethren, see that ye love one another with a pure heart fervently. 1 PETER 1:22

What will ye do in the solemn day, and in the day of the feast of the LORD? HOSEA 9:5

Grace be with all them that love our Lord Jesus Christ in sincerity. Amen. EPHESIANS 6:24

Therefore let us keep the feast, not with old leaven, neither with the leaven of malice and wickedness; but with the unleavened bread of sincerity and truth.
1 CORINTHIANS 5:8

For our exhortation was not of deceit, nor of uncleanness, nor in guile:
But as we were allowed of God to be put in trust with the gospel, even so we speak; not as pleasing men, but God, which trieth our hearts.
For neither at any time used we flattering words, as ye know, nor a cloke of covetousness; God is witness. 1 THESSALONIANS 2:3–5

Young men likewise exhort to be sober minded.
TITUS 2:6

For our rejoicing is this, the testimony of our conscience, that in simplicity and godly sincerity, not with fleshly wisdom, but by the grace of God, we have had our conversation in the world, and more abundantly to you-ward.   2 CORINTHIANS 1:12

Wherefore laying aside all malice, and all guile, and hypocrisies, and envies, and all evil speakings.
1 PETER 2:1

That ye may approve things that are excellent; that ye may be sincere and without offence till the day of Christ.   PHILIPPIANS 1:10

I SPEAK NOT BY COMMANDMENT,
BUT BY OCCASION OF
THE FORWARDNESS OF OTHERS,
AND TO PROVE THE SINCERITY
OF YOUR LOVE.
2 Corinthians 8:8

Blessed is the man unto whom the LORD imputeth not iniquity, and in whose spirit there is no guile.
PSALM 32:2

And in their mouth was found no guile: for they are without fault before the throne of God.
REVELATION 14:5

Let love be without dissimulation. Abhor that which is evil; cleave to that which is good. ROMANS 12:9

Wherefore gird up the loins of your mind, be sober, and hope to the end for the grace that is to be brought unto you at the revelation of Jesus Christ.

1 PETER 1:13

But let us, who are of the day, be sober, putting on the breastplate of faith and love; and for an helmet, the hope of salvation. 1 THESSALONIANS 5:8

For I say, through the grace given unto me, to every man that is among you, not to think of himself more highly than he ought to think; but to think soberly, according as God hath dealt to every man the measure of faith. ROMANS 12:3

DRINKING WAS
A SIN FIRST,
AND DISEASE LATER.
Billy Graham

Drunkenness, revellings, and such like: of the which I tell you before, as I have also told you in time past, that they which do such things shall not inherit the kingdom of God.   GALATIANS 5:21

Now therefore beware, I pray thee, and drink not wine nor strong drink, and eat not any unclean thing.   JUDGES 13:4

For he shall be great in the sight of the Lord, and shall drink neither wine nor strong drink; and he shall be filled with the Holy Ghost, even from his mother's womb.   LUKE 1:15

Wine is a mocker, strong drink is raging: and whosoever is deceived thereby is not wise.

PROVERBS 20:1

Woe unto them that rise up early in the morning, that they may follow strong drink; that continue until night, till wine inflame them!   ISAIAH 5:11

Who hath woe? who hath sorrow? who hath contentions? who hath babbling? who hath wounds without cause? who hath redness of eyes?

They that tarry long at the wine; they that go to seek mixed wine.

Look not thou upon the wine when it is red, when it giveth his colour in the cup, when it moveth itself aright.

At the last it biteth like a serpent, and stingeth like an adder.   PROVERBS 23:29–32

And they have cast lots for my people; and have given a boy for an harlot, and sold a girl for wine, that they might drink.   JOEL 3:3

Woe unto him that giveth his neighbour drink, that puttest thy bottle to him, and makest him drunken also, that thou mayest look on their nakedness!

HABAKKUK 2:15

And take heed to yourselves, lest at any time your hearts be overcharged with surfeiting, and drunkenness, and cares of this life, and so that day come upon you unawares.   LUKE 21:34

For while they be folden together as thorns, and while they are drunken as drunkards, they shall be devoured as stubble fully dry.   NAHUM 1:10

WHOREDOM AND WINE
AND NEW WINE
TAKE AWAY THE HEART.
Hosea 4:11

For the drunkard and the glutton shall come to poverty: and drowsiness shall clothe a man with rags.
PROVERBS 23:21

DO NOT PRAY FOR EASY LIVES.
PRAY TO BE STRONGER MEN!
DO NOT PRAY FOR TASKS
EQUAL TO YOUR POWERS.
PRAY FOR POWER EQUAL TO
YOUR TASKS.

Phillips Brooks

He giveth power to the faint; and to them that have no might he increaseth strength.   ISAIAH 40:29

Wait on the LORD: be of good courage, and he shall strengthen thine heart: wait, I say, on the LORD.
PSALM 27:14

The LORD will give strength unto his people; the LORD will bless his people with peace.
PSALM 29:11

For the eyes of the LORD run to and fro throughout the whole earth, to shew himself strong in the behalf of them whose heart is perfect toward him.

2 CHRONICLES 16:9

But they that wait upon the LORD shall renew their strength; they shall mount up with wings as eagles; they shall run, and not be weary; and they shall walk, and not faint.

ISAIAH 40:31

The LORD is my rock, and my fortress, and my deliverer; my God, my strength, in whom I will trust; my buckler, and the horn of my salvation, and my high tower.

PSALM 18:2

I know both how to be abased, and I know how to abound: every where and in all things I am instructed both to be full and to be hungry, both to abound and to suffer need.

I can do all things through Christ which strengtheneth me.

PHILIPPIANS 4:12–13

The righteous also shall hold on his way, and he that hath clean hands shall be stronger and stronger.

JOB 17:9

By pureness, by knowledge, by longsuffering, by kindness, by the Holy Ghost, by love unfeigned,

By the word of truth, by the power of God, by the armour of righteousness on the right hand and on the left.

2 CORINTHIANS 6:6–7

Both riches and honour come of thee, and thou reignest over all; and in thine hand is power and might; and in thine hand it is to make great, and to give strength unto all.   1 CHRONICLES 29:12

MY FLESH AND
MY HEART FAILETH:
BUT GOD IS THE
STRENGTH OF MY HEART,
AND MY PORTION
FOR EVER.
Psalm 73:26

That ye might walk worthy of the Lord unto all pleasing, being fruitful in every good work, and increasing in the knowledge of God;

Strengthened with all might, according to his glorious power, unto all patience and longsuffering with joyfulness.   COLOSSIANS 1:10–11

O God, thou art terrible out of thy holy places: the God of Israel is he that giveth strength and power unto his people. Blessed be God.   PSALM 68:35

And he said unto me, My grace is sufficient for thee: for my strength is made perfect in weakness. Most gladly therefore will I rather glory in my infirmities, that the power of Christ may rest upon me.
2 CORINTHIANS 12:9

Finally, my brethren, be strong in the Lord, and in the power of his might. EPHESIANS 6:10

Nay, in all these things we are more than conquerors through him that loved us. ROMANS 8:37

WE USUALLY KNOW
WHAT WE CAN DO,
BUT TEMPTATION SHOWS US
WHO WE ARE.
Thomas a Kempis

And lead us not into temptation, but deliver us from evil: For thine is the kingdom, and the power, and the glory, for ever. Amen.   MATTHEW 6:13

Watch and pray, that ye enter not into temptation: the spirit indeed is willing, but the flesh is weak.
MATTHEW 26:41

And when he was at the place, he said unto them, Pray that ye enter not into temptation.
LUKE 22:40

There hath no temptation taken you but such as is common to man: but God is faithful, who will not suffer you to be tempted above that ye are able; but will with the temptation also make a way to escape, that ye may be able to bear it.

1 CORINTHIANS 10:13

Blessed is the man that endureth temptation: for when he is tried, he shall receive the crown of life, which the Lord hath promised to them that love him.

JAMES 1:12

Because thou hast kept the word of my patience, I also will keep thee from the hour of temptation, which shall come upon all the world, to try them that dwell upon the earth.   REVELATION 3:10

LET NO MAN
SAY WHEN HE IS TEMPTED,
I AM TEMPTED OF GOD:
FOR GOD CANNOT
BE TEMPTED WITH EVIL,
NEITHER TEMPTETH
HE ANY MAN.
James 1:13

The Lord knoweth how to deliver the godly out of temptations.   2 PETER 2:9

TRUTH,
WHEN NOT SOUGHT AFTER,
RARELY COMES TO LIGHT.
Oliver Wendell Holmes

Jesus saith unto him, I am the way, the truth, and the life: no man cometh unto the Father, but by me.
JOHN 14:6

He is the Rock, his work is perfect: for all his ways are judgment: a God of truth and without iniquity, just and right is he.   DEUTERONOMY 32:4

That he who blesseth himself in the earth shall bless himself in the God of truth; and he that sweareth in the earth shall swear by the God of truth.
ISAIAH 65:16

Finally, brethren, whatsoever things are true, whatsoever things are honest, whatsoever things are just, whatsoever things are pure, whatsoever things are lovely, whatsoever things are of good report; if there be any virtue, and if there be any praise, think on these things. PHILIPPIANS 4:8

For the word of the LORD is right; and all his works are done in truth. PSALM 33:4

And for their sakes I sanctify myself, that they also might be sanctified through the truth. JOHN 17:19

These are the things that ye shall do; Speak ye every man the truth to his neighbour; execute the judgment of truth and peace in your gates. ZECHARIAH 8:16

And ye shall know the truth, and the truth shall make you free. JOHN 8:32

For the law was given by Moses, but grace and truth came by Jesus Christ. JOHN 1:17

God is a Spirit: and they that worship him must worship him in spirit and in truth. JOHN 4:24

Even the Spirit of truth; whom the world cannot receive, because it seeth him not, neither knoweth him: but ye know him; for he dwelleth with you, and shall be in you. JOHN 14:17

For the LORD is good; his mercy is everlasting; and his truth endureth to all generations.

PSALM 100:5

BUY THE TRUTH,
AND SELL IT NOT;
ALSO WISDOM,
AND INSTRUCTION,
AND UNDERSTANDING.

Proverbs 23:23

THE NOBLEST PLEASURE IS THE JOY OF UNDERSTANDING.

Leonard Da Vinci

Then shalt thou understand the fear of the LORD, and find the knowledge of God.

For the LORD giveth wisdom: out of his mouth cometh knowledge and understanding.

PROVERBS 2:5–6

If there be therefore any consolation in Christ, if any comfort of love, if any fellowship of the Spirit, if any bowels and mercies,

Fulfil ye my joy, that ye be likeminded, having the same love, being of one accord, of one mind.

PHILIPPIANS 2:1–2

The tongue of the wise useth knowledge aright: but the mouth of fools poureth out foolishness.

PROVERBS 15:2

Justice and judgment are the habitation of thy throne: mercy and truth shall go before thy face.

PSALM 89:14

When I was a child, I spake as a child, I understood as a child, I thought as a child: but when I became a man, I put away childish things.

1 CORINTHIANS 13:11

In the lips of him that hath understanding wisdom is found: but a rod is for the back of him that is void of understanding.   PROVERBS 10:13

With the ancient is wisdom; and in length of days understanding.

With him is wisdom and strength, he hath counsel and understanding.   JOB 12:12–13

Wisdom resteth in the heart of him that hath understanding: but that which is in the midst of fools is made known.   PROVERBS 14:33

But let him that glorieth glory in this, that he understandeth and knoweth me, that I am the LORD which exercise lovingkindness, judgment, and righteousness, in the earth: for in these things I delight, saith the LORD.   JEREMIAH 9:24

Evil men understand not judgment: but they that seek the LORD understand all things.

PROVERBS 28:5

But as it is written, Eye hath not seen, nor ear heard, neither have entered into the heart of man, the things which God hath prepared for them that love him.

But God hath revealed them unto us by his Spirit: for the Spirit searcheth all things, yea, the deep things of God.

For what man knoweth the things of a man, save the spirit of man which is in him? even so the things of God knoweth no man, but the Spirit of God.

1 CORINTHIANS 2:9–11

THE HEART OF THE PRUDENT GETTETH KNOWLEDGE; AND THE EAR OF THE WISE SEEKETH KNOWLEDGE.

Proverbs 18:15

But thou, O Lord, art a God full of compassion, and gracious, longsuffering, and plenteous in mercy and truth.

PSALM 86:15

For if these things be in you, and abound, they make you that ye shall neither be barren nor unfruitful in the knowledge of our Lord Jesus Christ.

2 PETER 1:8

Make me to understand the way of thy precepts: so shall I talk of thy wondrous works.   PSALM 119:27

And unto man he said, Behold, the fear of the Lord, that is wisdom; and to depart from evil is understanding.   JOB 28:28

Folly is joy to him that is destitute of wisdom: but a man of understanding walketh uprightly.
PROVERBS 15:21

The rich man is wise in his own conceit; but the poor that hath understanding searcheth him out.
PROVERBS 28:11

Teach me good judgment and knowledge: for I have believed thy commandments.   PSALM 119:66

The heart of him that hath understanding seeketh knowledge: but the mouth of fools feedeth on foolishness.   PROVERBS 15:14

When wisdom entereth into thine heart, and knowledge is pleasant unto thy soul;
Discretion shall preserve thee, understanding shall keep thee:
To deliver thee from the way of the evil man.
PROVERBS 2:10–12

For to one is given by the Spirit the word of wisdom; to another the word of knowledge by the same Spirit.   1 CORINTHIANS 12:8

Happy is the man that findeth wisdom, and the man that getteth understanding.

For the merchandise of it is better than the merchandise of silver, and the gain thereof than fine gold.

She is more precious than rubies: and all the things thou canst desire are not to be compared unto her. PROVERBS 3:13–15

They shall not hurt nor destroy in all my holy mountain: for the earth shall be full of the knowledge of the LORD, as the waters cover the sea.

And in that day there shall be a root of Jesse, which shall stand for an ensign of the people; to it shall the Gentiles seek: and his rest shall be glorious. ISAIAH 11:9–10

WHAT EVER DISUNITES
MAN FROM GOD,
ALSO DISUNITES MAN FROM MAN.
Edmund Burke

Can two walk together, except they be agreed?
AMOS 3:3

Let him seek peace, and ensue it.   1 PETER 3:11

Be of the same mind one toward another.
ROMANS 12:16

Now I beseech you, brethren, by the name of our
Lord Jesus Christ, that ye all speak the same thing,
and that there be no divisions among you; but that
ye be perfectly joined together in the same mind
and in the same judgment.   1 CORINTHIANS 1:10

Now the God of patience and consolation grant you to be likeminded one toward another according to Christ Jesus:

That ye may with one mind and one mouth glorify God, even the Father of our Lord Jesus Christ.

ROMANS 15:5–6

BEHOLD,
HOW GOOD AND HOW
PLEASANT IT IS FOR
BRETHREN TO DWELL
TOGETHER IN UNITY!
Psalm 133:1

AS LONG AS I SEE ANY THING
TO BE DONE FOR GOD,
LIFE IS WORTH HAVING;
BUT O HOW VAIN
AND UNWORTHY IT IS
TO LIVE FOR ANY LOWER END!
David Brainerd

Be sober, be vigilant; because your adversary the devil, as a roaring lion, walketh about, seeking whom he may devour.   1 PETER 5:8

I watch, and am as a sparrow alone upon the house top.   PSALM 102:7

Watch and pray, that ye enter not into temptation: the spirit indeed is willing, but the flesh is weak.
                                                    MATTHEW 26:41

Let thine eyes look right on, and let thine eyelids look straight before thee.

Ponder the path of thy feet, and let all thy ways be established.　　　　PROVERBS 4:25–26

He that dasheth in pieces is come up before thy face: keep the munition, watch the way, make thy loins strong, fortify thy power mightily.

NAHUM 2:1

I will stand upon my watch, and set me upon the tower, and will watch to see what he will say unto me, and what I shall answer when I am reproved.

HABAKKUK 2:1

Watch therefore: for ye know not what hour your Lord doth come.

But know this, that if the goodman of the house had known in what watch the thief would come, he would have watched, and would not have suffered his house to be broken up.　　MATTHEW 24:42–43

And then if any man shall say to you, Lo, here is Christ; or, lo, he is there; believe him not:

For false Christs and false prophets shall rise, and shall shew signs and wonders, to seduce, if it were possible, even the elect.

But take ye heed: behold, I have foretold you all things.　　　　MARK 13:21–23

And what I say unto you I say unto all, Watch.

MARK 13:37

Beware lest any man spoil you through philosophy and vain deceit, after the tradition of men, after the rudiments of the world, and not after Christ.

COLOSSIANS 2:8

LOOK TO YOURSELVES,
THAT WE LOSE
NOT THOSE THINGS
WHICH WE HAVE WROUGHT,
BUT THAT WE RECEIVE
A FULL REWARD.
2 John 8

Watch ye therefore, and pray always, that ye may be accounted worthy to escape all these things that shall come to pass, and to stand before the Son of man.

LUKE 21:36

Blessed is the man that heareth me, watching daily at my gates, waiting at the posts of my doors.

PROVERBS 8:34

But watch thou in all things, endure afflictions, do the work of an evangelist, make full proof of thy ministry.

2 TIMOTHY 4:5

WISDOM

WISDOM IS
THE RIGHT USE OF KNOWLEDGE.
Charles H. Spurgeon

Therefore whosoever heareth these sayings of mine, and doeth them, I will liken him unto a wise man, which built his house upon a rock:

And the rain descended, and the floods came, and the winds blew, and beat upon that house; and it fell not: for it was founded upon a rock.

MATTHEW 7:24–25

He that is void of wisdom despiseth his neighbour: but a man of understanding holdeth his peace.

PROVERBS 11:12

I wisdom dwell with prudence, and find out knowledge of witty inventions. PROVERBS 8:12

A prudent man foreseeth the evil, and hideth himself: but the simple pass on, and are punished.

PROVERBS 22:3

The LORD by wisdom hath founded the earth; by understanding hath he established the heavens.

By his knowledge the depths are broken up, and the clouds drop down the dew.

My son, let not them depart from thine eyes: keep sound wisdom and discretion.

PROVERBS 3:19–21

Whoso is wise, and will observe these things, even they shall understand the lovingkindness of the LORD.

PSALM 107:43

A good man sheweth favour, and lendeth: he will guide his affairs with discretion.

PSALM 112:5

He that handleth a matter wisely shall find good: and whoso trusteth in the LORD, happy is he.

The wise in heart shall be called prudent: and the sweetness of the lips increaseth learning.

PROVERBS 16:20–21

Who is wise, and he shall understand these things? prudent, and he shall know them? for the ways of the LORD are right, and the just shall walk in them: but the transgressors shall fall therein.

HOSEA 14:9

A prudent man concealeth knowledge: but the heart of fools proclaimeth foolishness.   PROVERBS 12:23

My son, attend to my words; incline thine ear unto my sayings.

Let them not depart from thine eyes; keep them in the midst of thine heart.

For they are life unto those that find them, and health to all their flesh.   PROVERBS 4:20–22

A wise man's heart discerneth both time and judgment.   ECCLESIASTES 8:5

Be wise now therefore, O ye kings: be instructed, ye judges of the earth.   PSALM 2:10

THE SIMPLE BELIEVETH
EVERY WORD:
BUT THE PRUDENT MAN
LOOKETH WELL
TO HIS GOING.
Proverbs 14:15

Say unto wisdom, Thou art my sister; and call understanding thy kinswoman.   PROVERBS 7:4

Wherefore be ye not unwise, but understanding what the will of the Lord is.   EPHESIANS 5:17

The law of the wise is a fountain of life, to depart from the snares of death.

Good understanding giveth favour: but the way of transgressors is hard.   PROVERBS 13:14–15

For your obedience is come abroad unto all men. I am glad therefore on your behalf: but yet I would have you wise unto that which is good, and simple concerning evil.   ROMANS 16:19

And they that be wise shall shine as the brightness of the firmament; and they that turn many to righteousness as the stars for ever and ever.   DANIEL 12:3

With him is strength and wisdom: the deceived and the deceiver are his.

He leadeth counsellors away spoiled, and maketh the judges fools.   JOB 12:16–17

And wisdom and knowledge shall be the stability of thy times, and strength of salvation: the fear of the Lord is his treasure.   ISAIAH 33:6

How much better is it to get wisdom than gold! and to get understanding rather to be chosen than silver!   PROVERBS 16:16

If any of you lack wisdom, let him ask of God, that giveth to all men liberally, and upbraideth not; and it shall be given him.   JAMES 1:5

My son, eat thou honey, because it is good; and the honeycomb, which is sweet to thy taste:

So shall the knowledge of wisdom be unto thy soul: when thou hast found it, then there shall be a reward, and thy expectation shall not be cut off.

PROVERBS 24:13–14

Howbeit we speak wisdom among them that are perfect: yet not the wisdom of this world, nor of the princes of this world, that come to nought:

But we speak the wisdom of God in a mystery, even the hidden wisdom, which God ordained before the world unto our glory:

Which none of the princes of this world knew: for had they known it, they would not have crucified the Lord of glory.   1 CORINTHIANS 2:6–8

I will instruct thee and teach thee in the way which thou shalt go: I will guide thee with mine eye.

PSALM 32:8

And if any man think that he knoweth any thing, he knoweth nothing yet as he ought to know.

1 CORINTHIANS 8:2

Inspirational Library

Beautiful purse/pocket-size editions of Christian classics bound in flexible leatherette. These books make thoughtful gifts for everyone on your list, including yourself!